Pr
Slice Of Life: A Self-Help Odyssey

"Lindal presents us with the intriguing tale of the life and adventures of "Rikki." The book is delightfully written, and fresh and energetic in its approach. But this is not just a great story, it is also a teaching vehicle that imparts psychological and spiritual wisdom to those who read it. These jewels are woven into the narrative with an originality and finesse that easily carry the reader along. One of the principal characters is "Old Soul," with whom Rikki has lively exchanges which are well suited to help seekers on their way. This partly autobiographical and partly fictional book makes great reading for the adventurous soul."

> **Adam Crabtree -** Transpersonal psychotherapist, and author of *Multiple Man: Explorations in Possession and Multiple Personality, From Mesmer to Freud: Magnetic Sleep and the Roots of Psychological Healing,* and *Trance Zero: Breaking the Spell of Conformity.*

"With the dramatic landscapes of Iceland forming the backdrop, Dr. Lindal weaves an enlightening understanding of life, death and spiritual evolution through dialogues with a spirit guide named Old Soul. Wisdom from leaders of psychology and spirituality is integrated into an entertaining whole. Let me add that spirit guides are very real, as over a period of 10 years I have had dialogues with an extremely intelligent and articulate spirit being named Ahtun Re, channeled through trance medium Kevin Ryerson. Much of what I've learned from Ahtun Re is consistent with Dr. Lindal's narrative, which I highly recommend."

> **Walter Semkiw, MD.** Author of *Born Again: Reincarnation Cases Involving Evidence of Past Lives, with Xenoglossy Cases Researched by Ian Stevenson, MD., Return of the Revolutionaries: The Case for Reincarnation, Soul Groups Reunited,* and *Origin of the Soul and the Purpose of Reincarnation. Dr. Semkiw is also* President of www.IISIS. net, an organization focused on objective evidence of reincarnation.

SLICE OF LIFE:
A Self-Help Odyssey

A practical perspective for thriving within
the trappings of the physical world.

To Rich,

— Enjoy the journey...

Rick Lindal, PhD

authorHOUSE®

AuthorHouse™
1663 Liberty Drive
Bloomington, IN 47403
www.authorhouse.com
Phone: 1-800-839-8640

Cover: 'The Leap'. Etching
Artist: Halldora Gisladottir. Kopavogur, Iceland.

Published by AuthorHouse   02/21/2012

ISBN: 978-1-4685-2397-3 (sc)
ISBN: 978-1-4685-2395-9 (e)

Library of Congress Control Number: 2012901070

Table of Contents

This book is dedicated to my heroic mother,
Amalia Lindal,
Writer, author, poet
(1926-1989)

Diary Copyright

So clean the words upon the printed page, so neatly
typed in safe accepted terms, so sterile now for other's
eyes to see – these scratch wounds of my heart.

—Amalia Lindal

About the Author

Dr. Rick Lindal has a bachelor's of science from the University of Toronto and a master's degree from the University of Guelph Ontario, Canada. He obtained a doctorate in psychology at York University, England, while researching emotional responsiveness in adolescents. He subsequently worked at a youth custody prison facility for young adults. He returned to Canada in 1986, where he directed an outreach program for mentally disturbed young adults at the Kitchener-Waterloo hospital, Ontario, before commencing work at Mount Sinai Hospital, Toronto, as a therapist for victims of the AIDS epidemic. He opened a private practice in the early nineties, where he specialized in existential psychotherapy as well as past-life and inter-life regression therapy techniques. He is currently in private practice in Grafton, Ontario, Canada. (www. dr-ricklindal.com)

Foreword

I was raised in Iceland, in the town of Kópavogur, adjacent to the capital city of Reykjavik. During my boyhood years and until the age of seventeen, I spent four or five months every summer working at a farm; first at my uncle's farm in the north of Iceland and later at a farm in the south of Iceland. I had an interest in parapsychology from an early age, and after entering university, I read every book I could find on the subject. At university, I studied psychology and received traditional training in cognitive/behavioral psychotherapy, family therapy, and group psychotherapy. Over the years, my therapeutic approach gradually shifted and was influenced by existential approaches to psychotherapy as well as spiritual perspectives. I received training in logotherapy (the existential psychotherapy approach of Dr. Victor Frankl) and in the techniques of hypnosis and regression, with a specific focus on past-life and life-between-life regression techniques. During this time, I also read extensively in the area of paranormal research as well as the numerous books by Jane Roberts's "Seth Material," Neale Donald Walsh's series, *Conversations with God,* and Dr. Michael Newton's books on life-between-life regression.

Over the course of three decades of performing psychotherapy, I began to formulate a synthesis of the existential and spiritual approaches, with some specific conceptual underpinnings that I felt were important basics for psychological health and for a reasonably successful opportunity in life. In this self-help book, I've tried to integrate these concepts through a storytelling that is partly fictional and partly autobiographical. The reader of this book is taken on the spiritual/existential odyssey of a young boy as he comes of age and develops into adulthood. The setting is a fairy-tale land of elves and trolls, and the boy's spiritual guide educates him about some fundamental principles of life. The book is intended for a readership of all ages, and especially to those who find themselves wrestling with existential questions.

A reader familiar with the existential theories espoused by the late Victor Frankl, by the discarnate entity "Seth," who was channeled by the late Jane Roberts in the sixties; by Donald Walsh's channeled *Conversations with God*; and by Michael Newton's writings on life-between-life regression will recognize the influence these authors have had in the development and shaping of this work, which is, in large measure, a synthesis of their concepts with the addition of my own. Because of this, and for fear of referencing these authors out of context, I have only made sporadic references to their work within the pages of this book. That being said, the concepts espoused by them are clearly identifiable throughout the book, and I acknowledge with gratitude their influence on my conceptual framework and on my therapeutic practice for the past thirty years. Their individual works are listed and recommended as suggested reading at the end of the book.

Acknowledgments

The author wishes to express his gratitude to Catherine Watson for her initial recommendations after reading the first draft. Special thanks also to Steve Miller, Mark Lindal, Tracy Henshaw, Dan Lang, and James Dart for their invaluable comments and suggestions after reading drafts of the manuscript. And last but not least, to my husband, John Van Bakel, for his enduring support and patience during the many hours I spent sitting at the computer typing away, when he wished I were more available to attend to pressing family matters.

Chapter 1

Problem Boy

T HE PUPILS TOOK TURNS reading, two paragraphs each, starting with the child seated at the beginning of the first row, followed by the one behind. Some were more skilled than others, but they all seemed to read with ease. Each time a child finished his or her section, Rikki knew his turn was coming closer, and his fear grew stronger. Soon it was Rikki's best friend Hugo's turn. Hugo sat in front of Rikki and read with lightning speed. Finally it was Rikki's turn. He was flushed and sweating, even though he only had to read four short lines—on account of his dreadful stammer:

"J-J-J-J-Jack and J-J-J-J-Jill went up the hill
To f-f-f-f-fetch a p-p-p-pail of water.
J-J-J-J-Jack fell down and b-b-b-broke his crown,
And J-J-J-J-Jill came t-t-t-tumbling after."

It seemed to take forever for him to utter these few words, while the class of twenty pupils sat in silence. A repeat of this ordeal took place every day throughout the school year.

The year was 1960, and Rikki was eight years old. He lived in the town of Kopavogur next to the capital city of Reykjavik, in Iceland. He was the second-oldest of four brothers. His father, Baldur, a chemical engineer, was distant and usually appeared to be preoccupied and deep in thought, puffing on his pipe while contemplating some scientific project that he was working on. His mother, Amalia, on the other hand, was warm and loving. She did the lion's share of the parenting while maintaining a career as a journalist and writer on contemporary life in Iceland. His parents were unfulfilled in their marriage. There was no alcohol abuse or unruly behavior between them; they were just unhappy in their relationship with one another. They had met while students in 1948 and had once been very much in love. Rikki's father was studying chemical engineering at MIT and his mother was a student of journalism at the University of Boston. They married within a year and left the United States to start a new life in Iceland. The adjustment for an American to Icelandic culture, however, had not been easy. By 1960 Amalia had given birth to four children, and she was soon to be pregnant with another. The stress of raising the family was evident for those who knew them well. Amalia earned some extra money as a foreign correspondent and spent every spare minute she had scribbling down notes about her new adventures in Iceland; these were later published in a best seller that continues to enjoy new editions to this day[1].

Rikki (bottom left) at age eight in 1960,
with his parents and three brothers.

Rikki had troubles at school. He felt ashamed and humiliated on account of his stammer, and for this reason, unknown to his parents, he was often truant for days on end. In those days, while attendance was taken in class, the school did not have a policy to notify the parents until after a child had been absent from school for a few days without an explanation. Inevitably, however, the school eventually notified Rikki's parents, at which time the "cat was out of the bag," so to speak, and Rikki was called onto the carpet for an explanation. The conversations often went as follows:

---

[1]   Amalia Lindal. *Ripples From Iceland*. New York: Norton & Company, 1962.

Mother: "I packed your lunch, and you left for school every morning. Where did you go all that time?"

Rikki: "I went for long walks, and sometimes I also watched the construction workers work on the new subdivision that is being built on the way to school."

Mother, exasperated: "Why, Rikki? Why do you do this? I'm afraid you will get hurt out on your own. It's very important that you go to school."

Rikki: "It makes me feel bad. I s-s-s-stammer and can't read like everyone else."

His mother felt terribly sad for her little boy, but she was frustrated too, as this was not the first time Rikki had been truant.

Mother: "Why didn't you tell me about not going? I would have helped you."

The sad fact was that his mother had not had the time to learn to speak Icelandic sufficiently in order to be able to help him with his reading and writing. She was stressed to the nines with looking after his brothers and with running the home. His dad was away at work all day, and Rikki found him frustratingly slow to explain things when he made attempts to help him with his homework in the evenings.

Rikki: "After the first day, I was afraid to go back. And then I was more afraid to go after that. And now I'm way behind on my school work . . . and it is even more scary to go back."

Rikki suffered from a condition that was in those days called "truancy sickness"; in other words, the longer you stay away from school, the more difficult it is to return. So, after long conversations and attempts to convince Rikki to return to school on his own, his parents were usually reduced to the last resort of dragging him back, kicking and screaming.

Mother: "I'm sorry, but your dad will have to take you back to school tomorrow."

Rikki, breaking down in a flood of tears and defiance, throwing a temper tantrum: "No, I won't go!"

Mother: "You must go to school like everyone else. Your brother goes. We have no problem with him."

Rikki: "No, I'm not going. I'm never going back to school."

Rikki usually remained defiant, and on the following day, his father, after further unsuccessful attempts to persuade him, had to pick him up and forcefully drag him out to the car, kicking and screaming. On these occasions, Rikki was first taken to the principal's office for a talk, during which his parents wrung their hands and his teacher explained to Rikki that he must return to class. Rikki was then led back to class, disheveled and embarrassed in front of his dumbstruck classmates, and shown to his desk. A subsequent meeting was normally arranged with the school psychologist, but it was to no avail; Rikki never said more than a couple of words to him. This same chain of events was played out on numerous occasions.

Rikki's parents did what they could to help him. Private tutoring was arranged. Rikki's mother walked him over to his teacher's home on weekends, where he'd spend a couple of hours receiving one-on-one help with his studies. Rikki was fond of his mother, and these brief walks became memorable, as he cherished the unconditional love he received from her—despite all the trouble he had caused. The truancy sickness began when Rikki was eight and it reared its ugly head on a few occasion every school year, much to his parents' sorrow, until he turned eleven.

Aside from the occasional temper tantrum when he didn't get his own way, Rikki was even tempered and in good spirits most of the time. He was helpful to his mother around the house and regularly volunteered to pick up groceries at the local store. His parents had a charge account at the store and his mother always wrote out a list of groceries for Rikki to pick up. On some occasions Rikki was naughty and added a bar of chocolate to the list. The problem was that his style of writing was markedly different from his mother's beautifully cultured New England longhand, and the grocery store attendant serving behind the counter could easily spot his clumsily handwritten addition to the list of items. The local grocery store was owned and operated by a single mother and her teenaged son, and the mother knew Rikki's mother well. When Rikki was unfortunate enough to land the mother as his server, she would immediately spot his anomaly on the list of groceries, become suspicious, and ask, "Did your mother write 'large bar of chocolate with raisins' on this list?" To which, if Rikki would reply, guiltily, "Er . . . yes," she would proceed to call his mother to double-check. These incidents were naturally a little humiliating for Rikki, so he always tried his best to land the son as his server, who didn't care, and always gave Rikki the bar of chocolate without question. This, of course, required vigilance, a bit of cunning and contrived diplomacy, and waiting for others in line to go ahead of him when necessary. On successful days when this effort paid off, he would wolf the chocolate bar down on his walk back home with the groceries.

Rikki also had a habit of stealing money from a small cash reserve that was kept on the top shelf in the kitchen cupboard for miscellaneous expenses. He'd use the stolen cash to treat himself and his friends to candy and soda pop. This activity, however, came to an abrupt end when one of his friends, jealous at not having been included in the treats, ratted him out to his father. On this eventful day, Baldur set out immediately and found where Rikki was gorging himself on candy. A talk-down and a spanking in front of his friends brought this clandestine activity to a quick end. Despite all of these faults, Rikki was a likable child; he was his mother's favorite and he always had at least one special friend.

By the age of eleven, Rikki was of average build, with dirty-blond hair. His stammer persisted, and he continued to have difficulty at school in all of his subjects. He didn't speak much to others because of his stammer, and he tended to keep to himself during school breaks. He didn't like to participate in sports, and he especially disliked gymnasium, due to his inability to control his erections while having communal showers with the boys following class. The school also mandated that all children learn to swim. Rikki, however, had a long-standing fear of water, and he usually managed to avoid the school bus that transported the children from the schoolyard to a nearby town for swimming lessons, which were also marked with the embarrassment of taking communal showers before and after the swimming lessons.

The Farm, Lakjamot

As was the custom in Iceland at that time, Rikki's parents made arrangements for him to spend the summer months on a farm. He was fortunate that there was an ancestral farm where he could stay, located in the north of Iceland, with his uncle, Siggi. So, from the age of eight, at the beginning of every summer, in the month of May, his father would make the trip in his Opel and deliver Rikki to the farm. The trip took them along meandering gravel roads, up from the lowlands of Reykjavík, onto the moors, and back down, through some beautiful valleys. On the way, they crossed many narrow bridges with gushing rivers that bellowed down steep mountain faces, some carrying milky glacial water from the snow-covered mountain tops, while others had clear spring water emanating from natural springs within the hillsides. On this occasion, Rikki had just turned twelve, and this would be the fifth summer he'd spend at his uncle's farm.

The farm, Lakjamot,[2] is located in Shrub Valley[3] in the north of Iceland and stands majestically on a mound, not far from Shrub Valley Mountain,[4] which Rikki's father nostalgically considered to be the most beautiful mountain in the land. Lakjamot is a well-known farm in the district and was the homestead of Rikki's

---

[2] Modified spelling for the farm Lækjamót, located in Vestur Húnavatnssýsla.

[3] Icel. name; Víðidalur.

[4] Icel. name; Víðidalsfjall.

grandparents and forefathers, dating all the way back to 1835. His grandfather, a geologist, and his grandmother, a writer and a women's rights advocate, had both passed on a number of years ago. The district's postal station, as well as the central phone station for the entire county, was located at the farm.

Along the main road, not far from the farm, there is a large river named Shrub Valley River[5]. The bridge over this river is old and narrow, but when Rikki's father lived at the farm as a boy, a different bridge spanned the river that was even narrower and sometimes dangerous to cross, especially during the melting of snow and ice in the spring thaw. As they crossed this bridge, Rikki's father reminisced that, while delivering mail to a nearby farm when he was twelve years of age, his bicycle had slipped on ice and tumbled over the side of the bridge. He fell twenty feet down onto the rock face that lined the banks of the river. Fortunately, as he fell through the air, his letter bag swung up, over his shoulder, and cushioned his head as he landed on the rocks. He lost consciousness when he hit the rocks. Baldur explained further, that as he lay unconscious, he was approached by an elf-woman who lived in the rocks. She saved him from death during the fall, and as she nursed his wounds, she muttered under her breath, "What I sow, so shall I reap, what I sow, so shall I reap, what I sow, so shall I reap." Sometime later, when he regained consciousness, he stood up and felt miraculously fine, despite his fall. Later that day, he returned to the farm with his mangled bicycle and, much to everyone's surprise, without a single bruise.

This wasn't the first time Rikki had heard of elves, commonly known in Icelandic folklore as "hidden people."[6] According to folklore, they inhabit large rocks and rock faces throughout the land and go about their business, usually as farmers, attending to their animals and making hay during the summer. They are able to see human beings, but humans are not able to see them unless they wish to be seen. They normally coexist peacefully with humans, provided

---

5   Icel. name; Víðidalsá.
6   Icel. term; huldufólk.

their homestead is not disturbed. Thus it is in Iceland, even to this day, that roads are built around large rocks where elves are thought to live, for serious injury and even death has frequently befallen workers who have attempted to move rocks that are inhabited by these beings.

When Rikki and his father arrived at the farm, Rikki was re-acquainted with his uncle, Siggi, Siggi's wife, Elin, and their three daughters; who were two and three years younger than he. Rikki usually had a smile on his face, but he didn´t talk to them a lot, in part due to his stammer but also because he was shy. Baldur, before making the trip back to the city, sat down with his brother, Siggi, for one of their typical conversations. Rikki wasn't the only one who thought that it was odd to see these two brothers conversing. They would sit in comfortable chairs at an angle and across from each other. They hardly uttered any words, but nodded their heads every so often while verbally acknowledging one another with grunts and nonsensical sayings. There were also long silences. Then they stood up and exchanged farewells. Afterward, they invariably reported details of these "in-depth" conversations to their spouses and family members, along with decisions they had made about issues that had never been spoken aloud. It was accepted, by their families and by those who knew them well, that their conversations were, for the most part, telepathic. Following this notable occasion, Baldur relayed to Rikki's mother, sometime after his return to the city, that, he and his brother had come to a decision that they should exchange Rikki for one of his brother's daughters, as he had four sons and Siggi only had daughters, and there would be no male heir to take over the farm. Baldur explained to his wife that Rikki had demonstrated in previous summers that he was a good worker, and besides, Rikki was hard for them to handle in the city. So, they had agreed that having Rikki work on the farm, under his uncle's tutelage, would, no doubt, be good for him and provide him with a good livelihood in the future. But this idea was greeted with horror by Rikki's mother, and she resolved that this would be his last summer at the farm of Lakjamot.

Rikki always felt sad leaving his mother and doubly sad when his father left, after having delivered him to the farm. His father, however, would usually return on at least one occasion during each summer for a weekend of salmon fishing, as a portion of Shrub Valley River belonged to the farm, and angling in the river cost him nothing. On these occasions, Rikki's father would always bring a care package from his mother that contained a letter, some candy, and fresh fruit. Rikki was obliged, though reluctant, to share the candy with his cousins, but the letter, signed, "Love, Mommy," was always special and heartfelt. At the end of one of these fishing trips, as his father was about to leave, Rikki hid in the trunk of his car while he was in the kitchen having his final cup of coffee before the drive back to Reykjavik. As Rikki was nowhere to be found when Baldur prepared to leave, everyone assumed that he had gone over to the barn to do some chores, so his father left without finding him to say good-bye. After a couple of hours' drive, however, Rikki began to bang at the lid of the trunk, alerting his father, who stopped the car and found him hiding there. On this one occasion, Rikki enjoyed a couple of nights at home, but there was little to do in Reykjavik, as all of his friends were also at farmsteads during the summer. His eldest brother was away at summer camp and his two younger brothers and his baby sister were too young for him to play with. So he returned to Lakjamot three days later on the public bus. These separations from his family during the summer months, which had begun when he was eight, were difficult for him to handle emotionally, and it hardened him; some would say that it helped him grow up faster and become a man.

Days of Summer

Rikki was made to feel welcome at the farm. The farmhouse was constructed in 1929 and made of concrete. The roof had three peaks that were painted red, and the exterior walls were a chalk white. The interior was lined with wood paneling, and the walls were stuffed with dried turf for insulation. There was a basement, a main floor, and a second floor that contained six small bedrooms, three on either side, under the peaks of the roof, separated by a hallway. A small electric generator provided light on the farm's main floor and in the basement, but there was no electricity in the bedrooms on the second floor.

The floors were squeaky when people walked along them, and, night and day, the whole house seemed to be alive with ghosts. To make matters more scary, Elin, the farmer's wife, reported that a ghost would often stroke the back of her hair when she walked along the hallway at night. (Rikki, however, was familiar with the presence of ghosts, as his home in the city was apparently built on an ancient gravesite. The noisy commotion of people conversing and lights switching on and off in the basement at night were not uncommon in his home.)

There was also a graveyard situated at the bottom of a slope in front of the farm, about 150 feet from the front door, where Rikki's grandparents and other relatives who had lived on the farm were buried. There were chickens in one of the basement rooms at the back of the farm, which had a ramp that allowed them to go outside to forage during the day. There was also a cow barn, constructed in the late eighteen hundreds, with walls made of boulders and turf and a sod roof supported by wooden trusses and rafters, situated at the bottom of a slope, about 150 feet behind the farm.

Rikki slept in a room under the south dormer, on his own. An oil lamp was placed on the night table so he could see to undress and read before sleep, if he wished. His cousins slept in the bedroom across the hallway. Mice were busy in the walls, and mousetraps were placed along the wall to catch the less fortunate ones who ventured out into the room during the night. The traps were usually sprung during the night, and the first order of business in the morning was to empty them. Siggi slept in a bedroom under the north dormer, whereas his wife, Elin, slept downstairs on the main floor, on account of Siggi's heavy snoring that thundered throughout the top floor and literally made the windows rattle in their window frames, as there was no caulking holding them in place.

Fortunately, Rikki was tired from working on the farm during the day, and he normally slept through the noise the mice made in the walls, Siggi's snoring, the spooky creaks in the house, and the occasional sound of ghostly footsteps along the hallway outside his bedroom door.

The days of summer passed quickly. The sheep had lambed, for the most part, by the time Rikki arrived at the farm. They grazed in the pastures around the farm and on any bits of grass they could find along the mountain slope alongside Shrub Valley Mountain, located a few miles behind the farm. There were a dozen cows that needed milking twice a day. Siggi also had a herd of over sixty horses, mostly mares that had been set free to roam the moors on the highlands for the summer. They were herded back in the middle of summer with their newborn foals so the foals could be earmarked, and this was always a very exciting time on the farm.

A man named Peter, who was Rikki's grandfather's youngest brother, also lived on the farm. He had contracted scarlet fever at a young age and never matured mentally beyond the age of ten or eleven. He had a long gray beard and was normally dressed in a striped shirt with old suspenders that held up his trousers. He had a hernia and would usually hold his right hand inside his trousers to support the rupture that had never been repaired. He was a rather sad man and somewhat obsessive. He spent hours walking back and forth, through the hallway and into the dining room, muttering under his breath, "Golden Waterfall[7] came today." He appeared to be referring to a news brief that was broadcast on the radio daily at noon about the coming and goings of fishing trawlers and cargo ships, which included a ship named Golden Waterfall. However, no one really knew why he referred only to the ship Golden Waterfall. Perhaps there had been someone special on that ship that he had expected to see, prior to losing his mind on account of his illness: A "someone" who never arrived.

Peter's main chore was to look after the cows, which included feeding them and shoveling the cow dung from the duct behind them. This was a strenuous job for an old man, especially due to

---

[7]   Icel. name; Gullfoss.

his hernia. The job required that he first shovel the dung into a wheelbarrow and then wheel it outside the barn and dump it into a pit. This could be a treacherous task, as there were occasions when two of the cows, whose stalls were located on the far end of the barn, had diarrhea and spewed their excrement horizontally while he was cleaning the duct behind them. Peter, however, never missed a day of work.

There was also a girl named Dora, an older cousin of Rikki's, who had been hired to help with housework over the summer months. She was seventeen, with shoulder-length blonde hair and a fair complexion. Her routine in the mornings was to assist with the preparation of breakfast and to ensure that everyone was fed and that the girls' needs were looked after. Breakfast usually consisted of skyr (a type of yogurt) or porridge. If there were leftovers from the previous day, these two dishes were stirred together to form a concoction[8] that everyone seemed to like, except for Rikki, who would gag if he was made to eat it. To make matters worse, sometimes a cold slice of pickled blood pudding[9] was thrown on top of this mixture for good measure, making it even more putrid. Following breakfast, some of the fresh milk that had been brought in from the morning milking was poured into small bottles with nipples attached. Much commotion then ensued, as half a dozen lambs that had lost their mothers during the lambing season were fed from the bottles outside the front door.

Dora would spend the better part of the day operating the switchboard. The switchboard consisted of 101 plugs with umpteen cables that needed to be pulled and plugged in rapid order, to link phone calls from the farms in the district to the rest of the country. She was a "pro," and she sat there for hours on end with a headset that provided her with a link to the rest of the world. All the farms in the district had a distinct call, usually a letter of the Morse code alphabet, which they churned in rapid fashion using a handle on the side of their wall-mounted phone boxes,

---

8   Icel. name for this concoction is "hræringur."
9   Icel. name; slátur.

when making a call. And, as all the farms were connected on the same phone line, they were all able to hear each other's distinct ring sequence. They could lift the receiver and eavesdrop on each other's phone conversations whenever they wished. However, a learned ear could identify the distinctive "click" from each farm, that was audible when the receiver was lifted off its cradle. Also, the quality of the phone connection decreased noticeably, in direct proportion to the number of people eavesdropping. When the connection became especially poor, one could ask courteously if those listening would please hang up their phones, in order that the voice on the other end could be heard properly. In those instances, every farm's distinctive click could be heard again as they hung up their phones—of course, without uttering a word. On the few occasions that Rikki called his mother, as long distance calls were expensive, he would simply speak in English, his mother's mother tongue. And, as nobody understood the language, everyone would hang up their phones in rapid succession, providing for a good connection.

Rikki's cousins were, as young children are, loud and raucous in the mornings. They all had long hair that needed to be combed and braided. This was a daily ritual that included tears for the eldest girl, who had especially fine hair that extended down to her lower back and became tangled at night and needed to be untangled, combed and braided every morning. Rikki's suggestion that she should cut her hair short was considered on the verge of being blasphemous and, of course, never considered.

All of Rikki's cousins were of very fair complexion whereas he, on account of his mother being American and of mixed racial background, had a swarthy complexion. Dora and Elin would often sunbathe in the afternoon alongside the south wall of the farm, where they found shelter from the virtually constant breeze that blew from the northwest. It annoyed them to admit it, but their attempts at tanning were for the most part futile and left them with a burn, whereas Rikki seemed to tan almost instantly. It seemed to them that he only had to look at the sun, once, to get a beautiful tan. This was perplexing to the two women, as they had never seen this before. So, on one occasion, believing that he must simply be dirty, they took it upon themselves to scrub his face and arms vigorously with a facecloth and soap, all to no avail and much to their chagrin. Rikki's darker skin, however, made him feel different and alone, and not as much a part of the family as he would have wished.

Every week, as the week wore on, Dora began to look tired. She longed for her boyfriend, Karl, to arrive and whisk her away for a weekend full of fun. By Saturday, her impatience with the children was palpable, and she could hardly contain her anticipation of seeing Karl. By three o'clock in the afternoon, Rikki and his three cousins were all waiting with anticipation, noses pressed up against the sitting room window, peering out onto the main road to see the sexy V-8 Dodge Coronet appear. Before long and very predictably, a cloud of dust appeared on the horizon as the Dodge approached, as if floating on the gravel road in a haze of dust. The car would appear to be zooming faster than the eye could see, until it reached the driveway to the farm, further up the road. Dora, by now was quivering in her shoes with anticipation, her cheeks were flushed, her voice had jumped an octave, and her lips were ready to land a big smacker onto Karl's as he emerged through the front door. Karl never stopped for long, only to say a hello to everyone, before getting back into the car with Dora and disappearing in a cloud of dust, en route to Hvamstangi, a nearby town where they, in all likelihood, checked into a motel for a roll in the sheets before preparing for a wild night on the town. And so it was repeated every weekend, the children leaning onto the windowsill, waiting to see Karl's Dodge Coronet zoom in like a jet in the sky, with a trail of smoke behind it. He was a dashing man, dressed in high fashion and blue jeans. His thick black hair was leaden with loads of hair gel, and he had nice sideburns and a coy Elvis type of smile. And Dora, smiling from ear to ear, with a twinkle in her eye, dressed in a tight miniskirt, a contoured blouse, and sensibly high heels (as she was a "sensible" type of girl), slid into his automobile, adjusted her beehive, and checked her makeup before she waved good-bye to the children's envious little eyes, as she drove off with Karl. It seemed to Rikki and the girls that they never got to go anywhere exciting.

In other respects, life on the farm was an eye-opener for Rikki. There were a couple of incidents that Rikki found especially difficult to comprehend and that shocked him. A boy in his late teens lived on the farm named Gunnar; he was the son of Elin, from a previous marriage. Gunnar suffered from a heart condition and he tired easily. He had a rifle and, aside from target shooting, he enjoyed shooting the whimbrels[10] and the common snipe[11], although these were endangered species. Rikki accompanied him a couple of times on his clandestine "sporting adventures" and observed that he sometimes only managed to injure the birds he shot at. He'd then go and catch them flapping about and put them out of their misery by ripping off their heads—an act he said he was forced to perform to relieve their suffering quickly. Seeing this horrified Rikki and caused much consternation, but he had sworn not to tell anyone at the farm, so he kept this a secret. Gunnar also had a dog named Kolur, who was old and suffered from arthritis and had to be put down. Gunnar, however, refused to allow another person to perform this deed, claiming that it was his duty as the dog's loving owner to shoot it himself. Agonized over having to perform this deed, he nevertheless resolved to carry it out and then cried afterward. Rikki found this incomprehensible. Following these incidents, Rikki avoided Gunnar. There was something missing in his personality, a missing screw that, no doubt, had to do with compassion.

Understandably, there were also animals slaughtered on the farm that were destined for consumption by the farm folk, and, while it was disquieting and barbaric to see chickens running around with their heads chopped off, and a calf, lamb, or the occasional horse slaughtered for food, Rikki understood that these practices were normal. They nevertheless served to harden him emotionally, and he grew up fast.

---

[10] Icel. name; Spói.
[11] Icel. name; Hrossagaukur.

The farm Lakjamot (Photograph: Vigdis Karlsdóttir, 2011)

The Land of Elves

The weeks passed by quickly during the summer months. During the day, Rikki's cousins would often spend their time playing among some large rocks on a hill nearby. Rikki would sometimes join in with them, as it was his responsibility to look after them from time to time. The playtime passed quickly and with much excitement as the children ran among the rocks, seeming to others as if they were at play with a group of imaginary friends. Siggi, Rikki´s uncle, being wise to world's unseen, assumed, although he could not see the children's playmates, that his daughters were either playing with their spirit guides[12] or with the children of elves that lived in the rocks, and he thought nothing unusual about that. His daughters, however, never disappeared into the rocks with their unseen friends, so Siggi thought that it was likely that their playmates were their spirit guides. But it was also possible that the elves emerged from the rocks and made themselves visible only to his daughters during their play. On one of these occasions, Rikki suddenly began

---

[12] For enlightening research on this subject, please see Tobin Hart; *The Secret Spiritual World Of Children. Novato: New World Library, 2003.*

to feel sleepy and decided to sit down and lean up against one of the rocks. At once, he seemed to fall into a trance. He then noticed that one of the elf children was crying, sitting alone up against a large rock. Rikki walked over and asked the elf-child what was troubling him, to which the elf-child replied that his mother was ill and that she might soon die unless he was able to help her. Rikki offered his help, and the elf-child took his hand and led him to one of the large rocks. Beside the rock grew a beautiful plant with purple flowers. The elf-child leaned down and picked a leaf off the stem of one of these plants and rubbed it between his fingers until the sap moistened his fingers. He then asked Rikki to bend over so that he could reach to rub the sap onto his eyelids. As soon as this was done, Rikki was able to see into the "world of elves" with the same clarity as he could see within his own world. He realized that the little elf's mother and her twelve children where the only elves that lived within this gathering of rocks. The rocks provided beautiful homes for all of them, with vegetable and herb gardens outside the front entrances and pastures in the back for chickens, sheep, cattle, and horses. The elf led Rikki into the rock and into a bedroom where his mother lay, near death. Rikki asked in what way he might be of assistance and she replied:

> "Twelve and twelve
> Your father, now you
> Two lives in peril
> Payment is due."

Rikki surmised that this was the elf-woman who had saved his father's life, many years before, when he had fallen off the bridge and onto the rocks on the banks of the Shrub Valley River at the age of twelve. And now, with Rikki the same age as his father had been then, a deed "in kind" was due. The elf-woman asked Rikki to fetch a pint of whey, in order that she might recover her health. She explained that the unfortunate circumstances were such that the only cow she owned was pregnant and would not be able to provide milk until after she gave birth. She was therefore unable to make butter or benefit from the medicinal qualities of the whey, which is a byproduct of butter-making, created when the fat separates from the milk. Rikki knew that Elin and Dora had churned butter that same morning and that the whey, which was normally given to the calves to drink in the evening, was still available. Rikki made haste and returned with a pint of whey, to which the elf-woman added some herbs. She then drank the entire pint. She thanked Rikki for his kindness and promised that she would assist him in obtaining some important advice that would aid him in his life among humans. The elf-child then led Rikki outside and wiped the sap off his eyelids, whereupon the elf houses immediately returned to their former appearances as large boulders, and the elves were nowhere to be seen.

A couple of weeks passed by before the elf-mother made contact with Rikki again. She appeared to him in a dream and said that she had spoken to a wise old friend of hers who lived at Heather Hill,[13] which was situated three miles away on the banks of the Shrub Valley River. She said that he was a spirit and went by the name of Old Soul. And unlike herself, who lives in the hidden world of elves, Old Soul is a human spirit who lives in the hidden world of spirits[14]. The elf-woman advised that Rikki meet with this spirit being. Once again, she thanked Rikki for his help and reported that the whey he had provided, together with the herbs that she had added, had restored her health completely. In parting, she recited the following verses and asked that Rikki contemplate them prior to meeting with Old Soul, if he decided to follow her advice:

> In your world,
> Where I see you, but you do not see me,
> You enter by birth and contend with a
> Physical universe of:
> Light, given by your sun
> Gravity, by your Earth
> Seasons, by your weather
> Contrast, by your senses
> All of which you must accept and live within

---

[13]　Icel. transl.; Lynghóll.
[14]　Icel. term; Sumarlandið.

And there is You:
Unique by nature
Driven to action
Unlike all others
Creating experiences
Stuck in time
Shackled by fate
A lifetime of aging

And you will learn about:
Love and fear
Anger and depression
Guilt and power
Until your inevitable passing
And reawakening
In the Land of Spirits

Rikki remembered this dream quite clearly when he woke-up the following morning. A couple of weeks passed. There was a routine on the farm. Siggi woke him up at six o'clock every morning, and, as the cows slept outside during the summer months, Rikki's job was to fetch them from wherever they had wandered during the night. During the months of May, June, and July, the sun only dipped below the horizon for a couple of hours, and the nights were dusk. Most creatures only seemed to sleep for two or three hours during these summer months, and in the early morning, numerous varieties of birds chirped and sang, and life all around, as far as the eye could see, was teeming with activity. The cows would often wander one or two miles away, sometimes across marshes and bogs. Fetching them usually took an hour on foot, but it was faster when a horse was available and Rikki could fetch them on horseback.

These mornings were beautiful, but walking alone, far afield, across marshlands where the permafrost had melted the peat from beneath the grassy turf, causing the marsh to undulate beneath his feet, was both scary and exhilarating for Rikki. There were deep, narrow creeks in these marshes that formed a spider's web of streams that allowed the water to drain into a small lake and, from there, through a deep narrow creek into the Shrub Valley River, a couple of miles away.

As he walked through this patchwork of marshes, Rikki always felt afraid. For some unknown reason, he had had a longstanding fear of water. He remembered when he was age five and six that he used to get into trouble at home after using the toilet and being too afraid to flush, for fear of seeing the water being sucked violently into the drain. As he continued to walk through the marshes, he held his breath. He felt light-headed. His heart raced when the turf gave way to the weight of his body, causing ripples to spread down below through the wet, muddy peat, like when a stone hits still water. What if he fell through into the abyss below? He was alone. No one would ever find him. On a more rational note, however, he was comforted by the fact that the grassy turf had not given way to the weight of the cows when they had, presumably, walked across it during the previous night.

Fortunately, the patches of marshland were sporadic along his path, and, eventually, when Rikki came close enough for the cows to see him, he would "moo" as loud has he could, and the cows would recognize him and realize that it was time to head home. Their udders were full in the mornings, and they looked forward to a couple of scoops of tasty grain while they were being milked. When they heard Rikki call, they'd come sauntering along in single file, with the most dominant cow leading the herd. Rikki drove them on, and when they arrived at the barn, each would proceed to her own stall. They knew their places well, having slept in them all winter long. By the time Rikki arrived, Peter had cleaned the dung channel, prepared the stalls, and thrown a scoop of tasty grain meal into the crib for each cow to eat while being milked. There was no electricity in the barn; a small window provided enough light, and the cows were milked by hand. Afterward, Rikki would lead them out to pasture, where they grazed until early evening, at which time they were herded back for evening milking before being led out once again for the night.

Sometimes, the cows would wander over to Heather Hill, where the elf-mother had said Old Soul lived. And, occasionally, they would wade across the shallows of the river and over to the banks on the other side, where the grass was greener. The river was deep in areas where it was narrow, and the current threw the cows off balance if they chose to cross in those places, forcing them to swim part of the distance across.

One morning, when Rikki arrived at Heather Hill, he found that the cows had crossed the river. He called to them and mooed as loud as he could, but they could not hear him, due to a breeze that blew his calls of course. On the banks, alongside the river and up against Heather Hill, was a gigantic bed of granite rock. Rikki decided to climb up onto the rock bed and call across the river from this vantage point. As he stood on the rock, the breeze suddenly picked up, changed directions, and carried the sound of his voice across the river, toward the cows that were grazing on the opposite bank. As soon as they heard him calling and noticed him waving his hands in the air, they began to make their way back across the river; some wading, but others having to swim part of the way.

Later that day, in the evening, after Rikki had gone to bed, he awakened from a vivid dream. In the dream, he was sitting on the rock bed at Heather Hill next to the river, waiting for the cows to wade back from the other side. Just then, a spirit being emerged from the hill and said, "I made the wind that carried your voice across the river and helped you fetch the cows, and I will help you again if you wish." Rikki surmised that this must be Old Soul who the elf-woman had advised he meet. Old Soul continued, "To visit with me, you must walk in circles on this rock; thrice clockwise, and thrice anti-clockwise. Then, stand still, facing Heather Hill, while thinking a loving thought, and a door to my world will open for you to see." Old Soul then vanished from the dream.

Rikki had not told anyone about the experiences he had with the elf-woman, and he decided that it would be best to keep this dream to himself as well, at least for the time being.

The days of summer passed quickly, and by August, the season for making hay was in full swing. Siggi cut the grass using an old tractor where the land was level and a scythe where the ground was uneven or had steep inclines. And, while the sun was shining, everyone on the farm, rake in hand, gathered in single file and walked swiftly across the field, turning the hay so that it would dry properly. They proceeded in this fashion from one end of the field to the other, up and back, until the hay in the entire field had been turned. Once dry, the hay was raked into rows, and Rikki, on a horse-drawn baler, gathered it into bales before it was pulled by a tractor into the barn for winter. These were fun times, though driven with haste while the sun was shining, so they would not be caught by a change in weather.

There were many horses on the farm—some were work horses, used for pulling wagons and hay balers, others were for riding and the gathering of sheep and horses in the autumn before the snow fell. Rikki owned a beautiful auburn-colored horse, whose name was Trust.[15] Rikki always rode bareback, as this allowed him to enjoy the sensation of the horse's power more fully, including the sweet smell of the horse's sweat, especially after a vigorous gallop. Trust was a reliable horse, and Rikki had great affection for him. On Sundays, Rikki often took his horse for a ride to the nearby farm of Kot,[16] where he visited with a friend. The route to this farm passed within a short distance of Heather Hill, where Old Soul lived.

Another Dimension

Despite a seemingly idyllic life on the farm, Rikki was lonely, and he often felt forlorn. He perceived that his life was hard. His childhood seemed to pass very slowly; he couldn't wait for his twelve-year-old body to grow older. He often worried about overcoming his stammer and his difficulties at reading and writing.

---

[15] Icel. name; Trausti.
[16] Abreviated name for the farm Þórukot.

Rikki often thought about Old Soul at Heather Hill, what the elf-woman had told him, and the dream in which Old Soul had offered to give him advice. He certainly had numerous questions he'd like to ask of Old Soul, so, after much deliberation, he made the decision to take this spirit being up on the offer and to go for a visit at Heather Hill. A couple of weeks later, on a Sunday afternoon, while riding home after visiting with his friend at Kot, Rikki stopped at Heather Hill to see if Old Soul would appear to him as he had said he would in his dream.

Rikki dismounted his horse with some trepidation, then stood still and steeled himself for a few minutes. He made his way onto the rock and walked in circles as Old Soul had directed—thrice clockwise and thrice anti clockwise. He then stood still, facing Heather Hill, with the loving thought of the affection he had for his horse, Trust, in mind. A golden plover[17] commenced to chirp rhythmically, "Bee-bee, bee-bee, bee-bee, bee . . ."

Time stood still. A brilliant bright light emanated from the hill, then a doorway emerged, and the entire hill appeared before him as a universe with thousands of souls alight in all the colors of the rainbow. The souls were in the form of orbs, and they seemed to be occupied with the goings-on in their world; they went about their business without seeming to pay any attention to Rikki. There were gatherings of souls in groups that appeared to form little communities, while other souls appeared to travel about purposefully between these groups. Rikki was, in an instant, aware of an infinite universe inhabited by thousands of souls. He saw this all at once, as if in a dimension where no space limitations existed.

Old Soul from his dream appeared and said, "Welcome to the spiritual dimension. Please come into my private study, and we will talk."

---

[17] Icel. name; Heiðlóa.

Rikki's legs felt wobbly with fear. He walked into the study and plunked himself onto a stool opposite a chair where Old Soul had made himself comfortable.

Old Soul said with a smile, "You are welcome. Have a seat!" Then he asked, "What troubles you, my young one?"

Mustering up some courage, Rikki replied hesitantly with a stammer, "I've been having s-s-s-s-some t-t-t-troubles."

"Don't be afraid to speak," replied Old Soul. "I know about your stammer."

Rikki felt instantly that Old Soul knew what had been troubling him. He had prepared himself to ask a few specific questions, so he said, "I have some questions I'd like to ask you, if I m-m-m-may?"

"Yes," replied Old Soul warmly.

Rikki gathered himself and said, "I am often afraid, I also feel different and alone."

Old Soul replied, "I understand. Tell me more. What makes you afraid?"

Rikki replied, "W-w-w-water. Why have I always been afraid of water? I'm afraid of rivers, and I'm afraid when crossing the bogs in the mornings when I fetch the cows."

"Yes. I can help you with that," said Old Soul. "But first, tell me what sorts of things make you feel different and alone?"

Rikki said, "M-m-m-any things . . . it's difficult to talk about."

"Well, start with something small that doesn't bother you very much."

"You know my horse, Trust? I began to ride him bareback and then a couple of years ago, everyone began to tell me I should use a saddle. I tried, but it never felt right. So, after a couple of attempts, I went back to riding him bareback, and I've never used a saddle since then. My friends think it's weird and tease me about it, but I don't care. But I wonder why I'm different in this way?"

"I see," said Old Soul. "Now tell me about something more important that makes you feel different and alone."

"M-m-m-y stammer," Rikki answered. "Why do I s-s-s-stammer when I speak? It's very humiliating, and it makes me cry. And why do I have problems with reading and w-w-w-w-writing? I'm far behind all my friends at school. I'm ashamed."

"Yes, I can also give you some answers to these questions. But I can tell you have one more question."

"Yes. Why is my skin darker than my brothers', my cousins', and all m-m-m-my friends? I don't want to look different. Sometimes I feel that I don't belong. It makes me feel bad."

Old Soul, leaned back in his armchair and said, "Hmm, let me think about this. First, I'd like to tell you how much I appreciate you having the courage to come out and visit me here and the courage to ask these questions. I know it's not easy for you to talk about this."

Rikki said, "I've never mentioned these things to anyone before."

Old Soul said, "Yes, I know. I also know that we will have many opportunities to meet and to get to know one another, if you'd like that. Do you remember the poem the elf-woman gave you in the dream?"

Rikki, smiling hesitantly, replied, "Yes."

"That poem outlines specific topics that I'd like to talk to you about. These topics deal with some basic truths about life, which, once you understand them thoroughly, will be of great help to you for the rest of your life."

Rikki responded with tentative enthusiasm, "Really?"

"I'll give you some answers to your questions, but before I can answer them specifically, you will have to understand a few general concepts about the nature of life."

"Okay."

Old Soul continued, "I know that everyone who is born in Iceland is automatically a member of the Lutheran Church. And I also know that next year you will be confirmed, along with all of your friends, as that is the established tradition. So, let me begin by giving you a little bit of background information about the nature of beliefs, since it's your beliefs about life that determine all your experiences."

Rikki, relaxing a little by now, was beginning to find this conversation interesting.

"Let me begin by way of this introduction: It's natural for all humans to seek and adopt beliefs about the unknown that give them an explanation for things that happen in life that are beyond their immediate understanding. These beliefs are usually spiritual in nature, and numerous religious institutions have formed around these spiritual beliefs, each of which advocates a slightly different understanding of the unknown. Most of these religious institutions propose that there is an omnipresent figure, or an all-knowing force, represented in the concept of a god. The basic tenets of all religions are essentially the same, in that they all spell out specific advice to their followers on how they should live together peacefully.

"The view about the 'nature of life' that I am going to tell you about is, however, not a religious one. It is a spiritual view. You can consider it as a 'backstory' common to all religions, if you will."

Rikki asked, "What is a spiritual view?"

Old Soul explained, "The basic idea of the spiritual view I'll be telling you about is that you exist simultaneously in a spiritual dimension, or what you might call a 'heaven,' and your current life on Earth is an educational trip that will provide you with an opportunity to learn about yourself, in order that you may eventually evolve spiritually."

Rikki said, "I've never thought about my life in that way. Are you saying that I have two separate lives—one in the spiritual dimension and another here on Earth?"

Old Soul responded, "Yes and no. Your life here on Earth is separate and a different one from the life you have in the spiritual dimension, yet you are the same soul and you exist simultaneously both here in the physical dimension on this planet and also in the non-physical spiritual dimension. But I'll be telling you much more about this later on."

"Okay," Rikki said, "But can I ask before you stop: What is the difference between believing in a religion and having a spiritual view?"

"Having a spiritual view of life is not necessarily the same as being religious. There are many religions, and they all have their own unique religious stories. What they all have in common, however, is a spiritual view of love and a dictate to their followers that they should live with others harmoniously."

"But I learned in school that Richard the Lionhearted went to Jerusalem to kill Muslims because they were not Christian."

"You are right. Not all religious people follow the spiritual tenets of their religions. The problem has to do with politics and power, both of which do not mix well with the spiritual tenets of religion. The politics and the different churches vying for dominance create divisions among them and their followers. It's important for you to understand that the spiritual values are not the source of conflict between religions; it has to do with the politics of power."

Rikki said, "I think I understand."

Old Soul continued, "There is also no conflict with having a spiritual view yet not being a member of a particular religious faith. But I'll tell you more about these issues later, if you like.

"Now, with this little bit of background information about spiritual existence, let me give you some answers to your questions. Afterward, I'll give you some homework about the relationship between your spirit and the physical world in which you now live, which you may study later."

Rikki said politely, "Thank you."

Rikki was relaxed by now. Old Soul's loving energy was palpable, and it seemed to infuse every sense of his being. He was anxious to hear what Old Soul had to say about his questions, as he had never voiced his concerns to anyone before.

Old Soul continued, "The answers to your questions about fear of water and your strong preference to riding your horse bareback relate to past-lives,[18] and the answers to your questions about your stammer, academic performance, and skin color have to do with your future, in your current life.

"The reason for your fear of water, including walking across the wet marshlands and crossing the narrow creeks, has to do with a past

---

[18]　All references in this book to having lived specific past lives are authentic memories from the author's own past-life regressions.

lifetime. You do not remember this, but you have had a lifetime in this area of Iceland before. You were a peasant around 1100 AD, when you met a sudden death by drowning in one of these narrow creeks. You were an old man at the time, and you slipped on the ice during the spring thaw while making your way across this same terrain. You tumbled into one of the narrow creeks and drowned. Your unconscious memory of this death is stimulated when you walk across these marshlands, and it is the origin of your fear."

Rikki was amazed. "Wow!"

"In answer to your question about riding your horse bareback—again, your liking for this stems from a lifetime in the early eighteen hundreds. You were an Indian in North America. You loved horses and spent much of your life on horseback, always riding bareback, as was the custom in your tribe."

Rikki asked, "What exactly is a 'past life'?"[19]

"You will become an expert on past lives later on in this life, and I'll tell you more about that later. For now, all you need to know is that you are a very old soul, and you have lived dozens of lifetimes on Earth."

Old Soul continued, "Now, let me give you an answer to the remaining questions relating to your feelings of being different and of being alone. Your stammer is self-

> Were an Asiatic to ask me for a definition of Europe, I should be forced to answer him: It is that part of the world which is haunted by the incredible delusion that man was created out of nothing and that his present birth is his first entrance into life.
>
> - *Arthur Schopenhauer*

---

[19] For more information on this subject, please see the following books: Joe Fisher: *The Case For Reincarnation*. Toronto: Somerville House Publishing, 1998. Hans Ten Dam. *Exploring Reincarnation: The Classic Guide To The Evidence For Past-Life Experiences*. London: Random House, 2003.

inflicted. You created this problem in order to suffer in this specific way."

Mystified, Rikki asked, "What?"

Old Soul continued, "Through this suffering, you have already gained a deeper appreciation for those who struggle emotionally then you would have otherwise. This experience will be very beneficial for you when you start your profession and begin to help people through their emotional problems as a therapist."

Rikki objects, "But I have plans to be a veterinarian when I grow up."

"Your love for animals will always be with you, and your work will always be focused on healing and helping others, but your focus will shift from animals to humans as you get older,"

Rikki was deep in thought. "I see," he murmured.

"Let me continue with my answers to your questions.

"In answer to your question about difficulties with reading and writing, this condition is also self-inflicted. It is a symptom of a condition called dyslexia. As with your stammer, struggling in this way with reading and writing will help you appreciate the hard work that is needed in order to overcome adversity.

"And finally, in answer to your last question, about being different due to your darker skin, this was also self-inflicted. You knew that the experience of looking different in this way would allow you to gain a deeper sensitivity for others who are dark skinned, as well as a deeper sensitivity for other races. This will also prove to be important for you in the future, when you work as a therapist."

This was a lot of information for Rikki to absorb. He felt stunned and bewildered. Old Soul could see from Rikki's astounded expression that his cup was full, so to speak, and that he had all the information he could handle in their first sitting.

Old Soul reached over and handed Rikki a capsule and said, "This capsule contains a 'thought bundle' in the form of a lesson. I will assist you in opening the contents of this capsule after you have fallen asleep tonight. I am certain that you will find it interesting."

Rikki took the capsule and said, "Thank you for seeing me and for all this information."

Old Soul smiled warmly and replied, "You're welcome."

Rikki's curiosity was awoken. As he was about to leave, he decided to ask Old Soul a couple of questions, and said, "Your friend, the elf-woman, told me that you are a spirit and that you live in the spiritual dimension?"

Old Soul replied, "That I am, and here as you sit in my study, you have a glimpse into the spiritual dimension."

Rikki continued, "My mother once told me that her father who died a few years ago is her 'fylgja'[20] and that he provides her with spiritual guidance by heightening her intuition when she feels unsure about certain things." "Is that what you do?" "Are you a fylgja?"

Old Soul replied, "Yes, I enjoy that type of work."

Rikki, now feeling enthused with the loving intent that emanated from Old Soul, asked, "Will you be my spirit guide, my fylgja?"

---

[20] Fylgja (plural; fylgjur) is the Icelandic term for an accompanying spirit who anticipates a person's fate, appears to the person and provides solace in harrowing circumstances, and serves as a guide throughout life. All people have a fylgja and those who are intuitively aware sense their presence occasionally. Also, a person may experience someone else's fylgja. A common example of this is the sensing or actually hearing the arrival of another person's fylgja one or two minutes ahead of that person's physical arrival. Pets, also, frequently experience the arrival of their owner's fylgja.

Old Soul smiled and replied, "Yes, if you wish. I will provide you with guidance in all matters in the form of encouraging your intuition, but I will never tell you what to do."

Rikki felt a weight lift off his shoulders, and replied with relief, "Thank you."

Old Soul smiled, "It is my pleasure."

Old Soul now stood up and said, "I think this is enough for our first meeting; we should call it a day."

Rikki asked eagerly, "Will we be able to meet again?"

Old Soul replied, "From now on, I will be your fylgja. But if you want to meet with me and have a conversation as we have done today, then you must come for a visit here at Heather Hill."

Rikki replied, "Thank you. I will do that."

Rikki stood up, and, as he turned to leave the study, a powerful force pulled him forward. Within an instant, he stood outside Heather Hill, feeling bewildered. The strange thing was that no time seemed to have passed. His horse, Trust, stood in exactly the same position. The chirp of the golden plover he had heard as the hill opened was uninterrupted, and it continued rhythmically, "Bee, bee-bee, bee-bee." Yet a mysterious meeting had taken place, and Rikki had acquired a vast amount of knowledge in a moment that appeared to have passed faster than the speed of light.

After taking a few minutes to contemplate what had just happened, Rikki mounted his horse and rode home. He had never heard of past lives before. He was also struck by the fact that Old Soul did not appear to be either male or female; the spirit appeared to have no specific gender. However, Old Soul was fully conscious and appeared to be as real as any other person he had ever met. The information he had received about past lives and about his fear of water and of bogs was helpful, as was hearing that he had been a

North American Indian in a past life. As he rode home and thought about having been an Indian in a past life, he recalled that his mother had once told him that she had documented proof that she was the great grandchild of Osceola's sister. Osceola was a famous worrier of the Seminole Indians in the Everglades of Florida in the mid-eighteen hundreds. His distant blood relative was Indian; he indeed had Indian blood running through his veins. This felt exhilarating.

As to Old Soul's answers to the other questions, these were more difficult to accept and not particularly helpful in the moment. Rikki had never thought of being a therapist or working with other people's problems. He had always wanted to be a veterinarian, to help injured animals. It also seemed incomprehensible to him that he would have elected to suffer with his stammer and dyslexia. Surely there must be easier ways to develop the attributes of compassion and diligence?

Rikki arrived home just in time to fetch the cows for evening milking. He didn't tell anyone about his eventful day at Heather Hill. Following supper, and after his chores were completed, Rikki went to his bedroom, lit the oil lamp on his night table, and lay in bed thinking about what Old Soul had said. A little later, after winding the wick of his lamp down until the flame went out, he drifted off to sleep.

The Purpose of Your Physical Existence

The following morning, before daybreak, as he lay in bed half-awake and half-asleep, Rikki opened the capsule that contained the homework Old Soul had given him. Within an instant, it was as if he had studied and absorbed the contents of an entire book.

This is what Old Soul said: "I am going to blast you with a lot of information, right out of the gate, that I hope you will adopt as a basic background for your life. These guidelines that I'm about to give you will help you thrive in your physical world.

"To begin with, as I mentioned to you yesterday, you need to know that you are a soul and that you exist simultaneously outside the confines of the physical universe within the spiritual dimension. This spiritual dimension is your permanent home."

"You are by nature a soul, which is a discrete self-aware, highly intelligent bundle of consciousness. Within the spiritual dimension, you have relationships with your friends and you spend your time pursuing whatever piques your interest. Learning about emotions is one of the topics you like to study, but, aside from the positive aspects of love, there is no opportunity to experience their impact directly within the spiritual dimension. In order to do that, you must travel to other dimensions. One such dimension is the physical world, containing the planet Earth where you are now enjoying a lifetime. Earth provides a grand theater for souls to learn about their inner natures and to evolve toward their ultimate potential. At the moment, there are three billion humans having this adventure in lifetimes that range on average from forty to eighty years, depending on where they reside on Earth. By projecting a portion of your soul into the physical world by way of a physical body, you are able to have direct experience with numerous events that are destined to take place on Earth during your lifetime. The emotional experience you create when you encounter those events will help you discover more about your inner nature.

> You exist simultaneously within the spiritual and physical dimensions.

> As long as you are not aware of the continual law of Die and Be Again, you are merely a vague guest on a dark Earth.
>
> - *Johann Wolfgang von Goethe*

"Shortly after your birth into the physical world, you induced amnesia about the simultaneous existence you have in the spiritual dimension. You did this to give yourself a clean slate from which to work while on Earth. However, intuitive knowledge of your life in the spiritual dimension remains with you. This intuitive knowing influences your waking consciousness and provides you with a sense of purpose and the motivation to engage in activities that you have set for yourself during your lifetime.

"Life on Earth is essentially about discovering who you are through creation; that is the creation of experiences that bring about emotions within you. The emotions you experience will have their roots in your relationships—with yourself, with other people, with animals, with physical objects, or with ideas. You are not privy to the details of the life you will experience beforehand, but you have selected all of the major events prior to your birth—the persons you will meet who will play a major role in your life and the places in which you will spend much of your life. You have also selected, for the most part, the types of challenges you will encounter, as well as a range of probable options that will be available to you to choose from when you find yourself in these circumstances. When these circumstances that you have selected unfold, you have the freedom to respond to them by making whatever decisions you like, because you have free will.

> Life is about discovering who you are through creation.

"Now, the main task you have during your lifetime is to learn from the emotional experiences that you create within yourself through encounters that will elicit reactions within you. By doing this, you not only begin to re-remember who you are (i.e., before your self-inflicted amnesia), but you also discover new aspects about your inner nature. This new learning allows you to evolve spiritually. This is the main purpose of this physical lifetime. After repeated lifetimes on Earth, and as you continue to re-create yourself in the image of your highest ideal of who you understand yourself to be, you eventually evolve spiritually, achieving higher tiers within the spiritual dimension."

Old Soul continued, "Now, consciousness permeates everything. Its basic constituent is the 'consciousness unit'.[21] Consciousness units combine in a myriad of manners to form all that exists within the physical world. They, for example, combine to form atoms, which combine to form the basic elements listed in the periodic table, then larger and more complex combinations of conscious forms that create cells, organs, and finally collections of organs that work together to form physical bodies, such as the one you now inhabit. This build-up of consciousness units, however, is finite. It is a build-up that proceeds through a cycle, from start to finish. For humans and for animals it is referred to as a 'lifetime.' At the end of a lifetime, these complex structures dissolve and return to their basic elements, only to recombine at a later time to form new physical structures.

"You, however, are a soul, and you are endowed with an infinitely more complex type of consciousness than what exists naturally within the physical world. Your consciousness exists outside the physical dimension of Earth, and it is eternal. It never dies, and it never dissolves into basic elements, as does the consciousness that forms matter and all life forms in the physical world.

"As I said earlier, a portion of your soul is projected into the physical world by way of your physical body. The larger part of your soul, however, remains in the

> We must walk in balance on the earth—a foot in spirit and a foot in the physical.
>
> - *Lynn Andrews*

spiritual dimension throughout your incarnation. This larger part, I will, from now on, refer to as your 'over-soul,' whereas the smaller portion that is projected into your physical body I will refer to as your 'soul.' Your soul, and the basic consciousness of your physical body that I just described, work together to create your 'inner identity.' Your inner identity, in turn, constructs the 'outer ego.' The outer ego looks out into the physical world. (As an analogy,

---

[21] Jane Roberts. *The Unknown Reality: A Seth Book. Vol.1.* New York: Prentish Hall, 1986.

the physical body, with its eyes and sensory mechanisms, is your motion camera into the world, whereas your outer ego directs this camera and determines what is recorded.) The outer ego is the hub through which all information is absorbed from the physical world and assimilated to form your initial impressions and opinions. It is your waking consciousness. The information it absorbs is analyzed superficially and funneled to the inner identity, where it is interpreted on deeper levels before it is passed on to the soul and onward to the over-soul. Information flows in both directions through all these channels, so the person is, at all times, receiving and sending information to the over-soul in the spiritual dimension and from the over-soul to the outer ego on Earth.

"So, to summarize: For purposes of discussion, you are essentially comprised of four aspects: (1) your **over-soul**, (2) your **soul** (3) your **inner identity**, which is formed through the amalgamation of the basic consciousness of your physical body and your soul, and, finally (4) your **outer ego**. The over-soul and the soul are your **spirit**. Your inner identity is your **unconscious**, and your outer ego is your **waking consciousness**. Now, try to visualize these different aspects of who you are as one large mass with very diffuse and fluid divisions.

"The first step your over-soul took to prepare for a lifetime on Earth was to communicate with the over-souls of your future parents and reach an agreement with them that they would be willing to conceive you. Your conception initiated a process whereby particles of basic consciousness, within the physical world, began to group together to form the human body you now possess. Your body has a physical image that is a combination of your parents' bodies, but it also bears striking similarities to bodies you have had in previous lifetimes[22].

---

22 For interesting research on this subject, especially with regard to striking similarities in facial recognition from one life to the next, see Dr. Walter Semkiw's books: *Return of the Revolutionaries*. Hampton Roads, Charlottesville, 2003, and *Born Again: Reincarnation Cases Involving Evidence of Past Lives, with Xenoglossy Cases Researched by Ian Stevenson, MD*. Pluto Project, 2011.

"Shortly after conception, your soul began to meld with the consciousness of the fetus, while forming your inner identity. During this time, your soul influenced what your fetus would ultimately look like as an adult, and began to form a working relationship with the fetus. During gestation, this relationship developed into a symbiotic relationship—that is to say, the body you now possess will not survive without the presence of your soul within it. It will die when you withdraw your soul. This symbiotic relationship is necessary for the soul to have a good working relationship with the consciousness of your physical body and to develop the inner identity, which is an important way station. This relationship also allows the soul to influence how the body grows during its lifetime and how it develops in all manners of speaking. It was during this period of gestation that you deliberately induced the developmental pattern in the fetus that caused you to stammer and to be dyslexic, which I told you about yesterday."

Old Soul then concluded, "As an aside, it may interest you to know that your soul is not contained within your body; it envelops your body, not the other way around. Its energy is most dense within your body, and it becomes more diffuse and dissipates as it extends away from your body, disappearing completely within a few feet. This is why you are able to sense the presence of someone standing close by, even if you have not detected them with your body's sensory mechanisms. Some people have the ability to see this radiant energy field of the soul, often referred to as an aura."

This was the end of Rikki's "homework."

—◆◈◆—

Despite the complexity of the concepts in this lesson, Rikki, at the age of twelve, internalized, remembered, and understood this information at a conscious level, as if nothing could be more natural. His soul and over-soul clearly had a working hand in making this information perfectly understandable. This knowledge began to influence the way he looked at the world and at everything in it, and it provided the beginning of a framework for how he viewed his life.

As with his meeting with the elf-woman, Rikki opted not to talk to anyone about meeting Old Soul or about his waking dream, at least for the time being.

Chapter 2

Summer Bliss and Spirit Entities

L IFE ON THE FARM continued normally. There were many interesting chores. One of these was to take the cows over to the nearest farm, Sel,[23] when they came into heat, as there were was no bull at Lakjamot to mate with them. On those occasions Siggi would strap a bridle made of rope onto the cow´s head and lead her across rolling hills and marshland, while Rikki drove the cow from behind. The walk over to Sel took a couple of hours. During these treks, Siggi and Rikki were often silent for long periods while they drank in the beautiful scenery of the rolling hills, some of which were weathered on top, exposing sections of gravel. The hills were surrounded with tufts of grass and Artic flowers, interspersed with swaths of blackberry and blueberry foliage and reddish-purple belts of heather. There were birds of all sorts flying about among the foliage—the most beautiful of all was the golden plover, and they also saw the common snipe, the whimbrels, pied wagtails[24] and northern wheatears[25], as well as the occasional ravens perched on a rock with blue-black droppings on the rock due to all the fresh blackberries they had eaten. There were occasional swarms of gnats, the odd fly, and some butterflies, but due to an almost constant northwesterly breeze in that area of the country, these were blown away before they could become a nuisance. The odd spider could be seen busily running about in the heather, but there were no insects that bit. Rikki could see for miles over fells, toward some mountains in the far distance, as there were no trees that blocked the sightline. His mind wandered, and as Rikki drove the cow, who hesitated to cross small obstacles such as streams and patches of marsh, it occurred to him that he should tell Siggi about his recent experiences with the elf-woman and about Old Soul in Heather Hill. He knew that Siggi had a keen interest in these matters and that he was well-read on the topics of spiritual issues and about beings in hidden dimensions.

---

[23]   Sel is a fictional name for the farm of Þorkelsstaðir.
[24]   Icel. name; Maríuerla.
[25]   Icel. name; Steindepill.

Rikki introduced this conversation by saying, "I met my 'fylgja' a few days ago."

Siggi responded, "That's good to hear. All men have a fylgja, but not many have had the fortune to meet with them in person. How did that come about?"

Rikki related the story of how he had met the elf-woman in the rocks behind the farm and what she had said about saving his father from a certain death when he fell off the bridge crossing Shrub Valley River, when he was twelve.

Siggi recalled this event and said, "Yes, I remember when that happened to my little brother. We were all amazed when he came home without having sustained a single scratch or a bruise during the fall. He never spoke about an elf-woman, but I have no doubt that elves live in those rocks under that bridge."

Rikki continued, "The elf-woman was near death when I came to her bedside, and she asked for a drink of whey, which I brought to her. It saved her life."

Siggi said, "You did well to help her, as refusing to pay a debt to an elf would have caused you untold suffering."

Rikki, building up some enthusiasm and confidence, continued, "She later introduced me to my fylgja, who told me about the spirit world and about two of my past lives. My fylgja also told me that I am a soul and that my soul is a projection from my over-soul that exists simultaneously within the spiritual dimension. My soul is eternal and it will never die."

Siggi was introspective and said, "You are already familiar with Earth, the Land of Humans, in which we now dwell, and it is good that you now are also acquainted with the Land of Spirits. This truth about simultaneous existence within different dimensions is not easy for many folk to accept, but now that you know this at your young age, it will serve you well. Do you know who your fylgja is?"

Rikki said, "No, I don't. This spirit being seems familiar, and seems to know me."

Siggi replied, "That sounds good. I think I understand." After a brief silence, while they wrestled with encouraging the cow to cross a small stream, Siggi continued, "Spirit guides certainly exist. There are also spirits who pretend to be guides. Some are malevolent, but most of them are spirits of deceased individuals who are lost and whose intent is not to cause harm."

Rikki asked, "What do you mean?"

Siggi answered, "Fylgjur are usually close relatives who have passed over into the spirit world. They might, for example, be your grandmother or your grandfather. They often come and play with their grandchildren when they see that they are lonely, and they look to protect them from harm. There are, however, also imposters who pretend to be fylgjur. These entities have selfish intentions. They are able to travel back in time and obtain personal information about you that enables them to pretend to be someone they are not, such as your grandmother or someone you cared deeply about that has passed over. They then endear themselves to the unsuspecting person under false pretenses, pretending to be someone they are not[26]. The initial introduction often occurs through the Ouija board or through a medium, where the unsuspecting person invites the spirit to speak to them. As this relationship develops over a period of time, the spirit manages to attach itself to the person's aura and then to experience the person's physical world by way of his or her body. The spirit then gradually begins to exert its will onto the unsuspecting person, telling him what to do and what not to

---

[26] For further reading on this subject, see Edith Fiore. *The Unquiet Dead*. New York: Ballantine, 1987.

do. The person may begin to experience periods when the spirit's personality is in complete control of the body."

Rikki said, "That sounds freaky."

Siggi said, "Yes it is, but it is true. There are a lot of documented cases of this happening. This type of spirit always has selfish intentions and you must distance yourself from them."

Rikki wondered, "How do I recognize this type of spirit?"

Siggi answered, "There is a way to distinguish between your fylgja and a malevolent spirit. The surest way to recognize your fylgja is that he or she will never try to control you or to tell you what to do. Fylgjur only offer their advice in an attempt to guide you. That's why they are seen as guides. A malevolent spirit, on the other hand, is demanding and attempts to control you.

Rikki said, "I will keep that in mind as I get to know my fylgja better."

Siggi responded, "Please come and talk to me if you ever have any doubts."

Rikki asked, "Are these bad spirits devils? Are they in hell?"

Siggi said, "God is all that is, including hell, if that actually exists. All humans are children of God, but, as you know, children don't always behave. Sometimes they learn by misbehaving and suffering the consequences of their own actions. These malevolent spirits used to be human beings in the past. Maybe they committed acts out of anger that they knew were wrong, and now they continue to suffer feelings of guilt and anger, which they take out on innocent people. God does not create hell for spirits, but spirits are able to create it for themselves, in their thoughts. These spirits are likely in a 'self-imposed' hell, which must be a frightening and lonely place to be."

Rikki said, "This all sounds really spooky. What about ghosts? I think I sometimes hear someone walking in the hallway outside my bedroom door at night."

Siggi answered, "Yes, my wife has also told me she's felt someone stroking the back of her hair on a few occasions when she walks up the stairs and along the hallway alone at night. I don't know much about ghosts, other than that they are not complete souls. A ghost is a fragment of a soul that was left behind when the main portion of the soul left the body at the time of death to join with the over-soul. This fragment of the soul feels it cannot leave, and it stays behind because of unfinished business on the Earth plane. They are not at rest and wander about, feeling agitated or upset for various reasons. This may occur, for example, due to unresolved guilt over acts they committed during their lives or because of unresolved issues relating to their dead bodies that may have been violated or not properly buried. Ghosts sometimes torment the living in an attempt to catch their attention."

Rikki asked, "So, in addition to fylgjur, there are also malevolent spirits and ghosts?"

Siggi said, "Yes, that's life. When we complete our lifetimes on Earth, it's not always easy for everyone to find their way back home to the spiritual dimension."

Rikki had much to think about. He felt relief at having told his uncle about his experiences with the elves and about having met his fylgja. But this seemed to open up a new can of worms. He was beginning to realize that there was much more to life than he had initially assumed.

Rikki and Siggi arrived at the cattle gate at the southern outskirts of Sel and proceeded toward the farm along a gravel path that led past some fields. The farmer at Sel greeted them when they arrived and led them to the barn. The bull was led out of its stall by a ring in its nose and introduced to the cow, who miraculously bore the weight of the one-ton bull when it mounted her, thrusting and grunting all the while. Once the bull had fulfilled its obligation, it was led away, and the cow was given an opportunity to recover. Meanwhile, the farmers and Rikki enjoyed afternoon tea and warm gingerbread cookies that the farmer's wife had just pulled out of her oven. After the refreshments, Rikki and Siggi set out on their trek with the cow back to Lakjamot.

It was mid-afternoon by this time. As they led the cow back down the gravel path, Siggi picked up their conversation where they had left off and said, "Our physical world here on Earth and our home-world in the spiritual dimension, I know exist. I am less certain about the dimension containing the Land of Elves, although our folklore is rife with tales such as the one you mentioned earlier. In these tales, elves assist humans in distress and humans assist elves in similar circumstances. The elves, however, always expect something in return for their efforts and are vengeful if they do not get it—but they also reward those who assist them, often handsomely, with gifts and good fortune."

Siggi continued, "Then there are the giant trolls who live in the 'unknown,' far away in mountains uninhabitable to humans. Have you ever heard tales of the giant trolls?"

Rikki said, "I have heard of the troll-woman named Grila and her husband, Leppaludi,[27] who come on Christmas Eve and spank children who have been naughty. They steal the ones who have been especially bad. I've been told that they stuff them into a huge bag and take them far away into a cave in the mountain, where they feed them to their hungry children."

Siggi said, "Yes, the folktales concerning the giant trolls center around the struggle with Christianity that was adopted by many Icelanders and imposed onto 'non-believers' around 1100 AD, about 900 years ago. The tales usually describe troll-women who

---

27   Icel. names; Gríla and Leppalúði.

torment priests and god-fearing people when they attend church or participate in common religious holidays, such as Christmas. There is, however, the tale of the cow named Boo-Kolla. This one may be fitting for me to tell you today. Have you heard this tale?"

Rikki, familiar with Siggi's knowledge of folklore and love of telling stories, said that he had not heard of the cow Boo-Kolla. He looked forward to hearing a scary tale to help pass the time on their walk home to Lakjamot.

Siggi began his story, weaving it into landmarks within the local district and adding his own version of events to the tale, so as to make it as scary as he possibly could.

The Tale of Boo-Kolla[28]

There once was a farmer who lived with his wife and only son at Kot—the little farm you visit on Sundays to see your friend. They only had one cow, whose name was Boo-Kolla. The tale begins one day when Boo-Kolla had just calved. Later on that same day, Boo-Kolla and the calf disappeared, and they were nowhere to be found. After the farmer and his wife looked for them far and wide, to no avail, they sent their only son, with some provisions of food and a new pair of shoes, into the unknown to look for the cow and her newborn calf. The son walked far and wide—through valleys and over moors and mountains—until he was deep into the highlands. By that time he was tired, so he sat down and ate some of the provisions his parents had prepared for him. After he ate his fill, he got up and called, "Moo now, Boo-Kolla, if you are anywhere alive." He heard the cow moo from somewhere far away. He walked in that direction for some time and sat down again for something to eat. Afterward, he stood up and called again, "Moo now, Boo-Kolla, if you are anywhere alive." He again heard the cow moo, a little closer than before. He continued to walk in that direction. He walked for a few hours and sat down for the third

---

[28] This tale is a variation on the classic Icelandic folktale about a mythological cow named Búkolla.

time, this time at the top of a large fell named Thief Fell,[29] which is located between Long Glacier[30] and King's Palace Glacier[31] in the center of Iceland. After some rest and nourishment, he stood up at the edge of a steep hill and called for the third time, "Moo now, Boo-Kolla, if you are anywhere alive." To his amazement, he heard the cow moo right beneath his feet. As he looked around, he found a sheep's path that led down a cliff's edge on the north side of the fell. He followed the path until he came to a large cave, where he found Boo-Kolla tethered to a stall. Beside the cow there was a large cauldron that contained the remains of soup that had recently been consumed, including the bones of a calf. Further back in the cave, he could see where a giant troll-women and her daughter slept and snored loudly. The boy surmised that the trolls had killed Boo-Kolla´s calf and made the soup and then milked the cow and drank the rich milk that was intended for the calf. They, no doubt, had plans to eat Boo-Kolla as well, for their next meal.

The boy quietly released the cow and led her up onto the cliff's edge and proceeded homeward as fast as the cow would walk. When he had walked some ways, he looked back and saw where the two giant troll-women emerged over the cliff's edge and came toward him. Their steps sounded like thunder as they hit the ground running. He realized that with their gigantic strides, they would soon catch up to him. So he said, "My dear Boo-Kolla, what do we do now?"

Boo-Kolla answered and said, "Take a hair from my tail, and lay it on the ground." This he did, and Boo-Kolla said to the hair:

> "This I lay, and this I say
> Be a mighty lake, I pray
> That only birds may fly this way."

The hair turned at once into a large lake. When the troll-women came to the lake, the larger one called to the boy and said, "This

---

29   Icel. name; Þjófafell.
30   Icel. name; Langijökull.
31   Icel. name; Hofsjökull.

will not do, and soon I shall have Boo-Kolla back." She then said to her daughter, "Go back home and fetch your father's large bull." The troll-girl ran off and soon returned with a gigantic bull who, at once, drank the lake dry.

The boy looked back and saw that the trolls were back on the run and that they would soon catch up with him again. So he said, "My dear Boo-Kolla, what do we do now?"

Boo-Kolla answered and said, "Take a hair from my tail, and lay it on the ground." This he did, and Boo-Kolla said to the hair:

> "This I lay, and this I say,
> Be a fire so fierce, I pray
> That only birds may fly this way."

And at once, the hair became a raging fire. When the troll-women came to the fire, the larger one called once again to the boy, "This will not do, and soon I shall have Boo-Kolla back." She then asked her daughter, once again, to go back home and fetch her father's bull and bring it to the fire, which she did. The bull now peed all the water it had drunk from the lake onto the fire and put it out. Again, the trolls set off after the boy, now taking long strides as they jumped from one mountain peak to the other, giggling with joy, thinking they had outwitted the boy.

The boy hurried along with Boo-Kolla and headed off the highland, down through Water Valley,[32] which is situated east of Shrub Valley where Lakjamot is located, intending to make his way home to Kot along Shrub Valley. However, as he entered Water Valley, he saw that the troll-women stood on the mountain ridge of Swine Mountain,[33] which overlooks the valley. They proceeded to pee into the valley with such volume that the riverbanks of the gentle stream that normally flowed down through the valley overflowed and gushed violently, making it treacherous for the boy and Boo-Kolla to proceed.

---

[32]   Icel. name; Vatnsdalur.
[33]   Icel. name; Svínadalsfjall.

Once again, the boy asked, "My dear Boo-Kolla, what do we do now?"

Boo-Kolla again answered, "Take a hair from my tail, and lay it on the ground." This he did, and Boo-Kolla said to the hair:

"This I lay, and this I say,
Be lightning and thunder so fierce, I pray
That only birds may fly this way."

And at once, the hair became lightning and thunder, causing bolts of lightning to hit at the source of the flowing waters. The shock of the lightning bolt flung the trolls onto their backs, and fear of the roaring thunder caused them to retreat. The boy now heard the larger troll call out in agony and in anger, "This will not do, and soon I shall have Boo-Kolla back."

The valley now became passable, and the boy made his way through Water Valley and headed toward his home at Kot. A few hours passed before the trolls recovered and began to run toward him again. The boy's trek home with Boo-Kolla was nearing its end, and he could see the farm Lakjamot, some distance away on his right and his home, Kot, some ways up ahead. The boy looked back and saw that the trolls would soon catch up with him, as they thundered along with very long strides. So, once again, he said, "My dear Boo-Kolla, what do we do now?"

Boo-Kolla answered and said, "Take a hair from my tail, and lay it on the ground." This he did, and Boo-Kolla said to the hair:

"This I lay, and this I say,
Be a mountain steep, I pray
That only birds may fly this way."

And at once, the hair turned into a huge mountain that is now known as Shrub Valley Mountain and stands majestically behind Lakjamot. When the trolls came to the mountain, the larger one called to the boy, "This will not do, and soon I shall have Boo-Kolla back." She then said to her daughter, "Bring your father's big drill, and we will drill through the mountain." She then added, "and don´t forget to bring the large soup cauldron, as the boy will prove to be a tasty meal, after this arduous day." The troll-girl ran home and returned with her father's drill and the soup cauldron, whereupon the troll woman began to drill through the mountain. She soon could see through the hole to the other side, where the boy and Boo-Kolla had almost reached the greens that surrounded Kot. At this, she became so impatient that she threw the drill aside and squeezed herself into the hole, stretching her arms through to the other side, while the troll-girl worked at pushing her through by the feet. But the hole was too narrow, and the troll-woman became stuck and turned into stone. After witnessing this state of affairs, the troll-girl began to cry, and she returned home to her father with the cauldron and the drill in hand.

Sometime later, while grazing in a field, Boo-Kolla saw the giant bull drinking at the shore of a wide fjord, located some distance away. Recalling the danger this bull had posed when the troll women employed it to foil her magic, Boo-Kolla took the opportunity to cast a magic spell that instantly turned the bull into stone. To this day, the forty-foot-tall image of the bull continues to be plain for all to see who pass along the shore of this fjord.[34]

---

[34] A reference to the rock formation named Hvítsekkur in Húnaflói.

The giant bull turned to stone (Photograph; Rick Lindal, 2011)

Rikki and Siggi had almost arrived home by the time Siggi finished telling his tale, and, as they headed down the driveway to the farm, Siggi concluded his storytelling by telling Rikki that his grandfather, who had been a geologist and researched the geological formations in Shrub Valley Mountain, had discovered the location where the hands and wrists of the troll protruded from a cliff's edge, halfway up the face of the mountain, and he had also discovered where the toes and feet of the troll could be seen sticking out from the other side. Siggi said to Rikki, "You are welcome to walk over to the mountain sometime and inspect this evidence for yourself, if you dare."

Rikki and Siggi had arrived just in time for preparations for the evening milking.

After hearing this tale, Rikki often found himself peering at Shrub Valley Mountain to see if he could make out exactly where the hands of the troll—woman could be seen among the rock formations on the face of the mountain, but he never ventured to look for her feet and toes on the other side.

Life on the farm continued its normal course. September rolled around. The sheep were gathered from the highlands, and the young were separated from their mothers and nearly all sent to the slaughterhouse. The horses were herded off the highland moor in October, and most of the foals were also sent to slaughter, for valued horsemeat. Horsemeat was a popular meat in Iceland, and Rikki's family normally purchased an entire foal, which his mother prepared for the freezer.

By this time, the cows were kept indoors at night, due to ground frost, so Rikki didn't have to fetch them in the mornings. The fall was both a beautiful and a sad time of year for Rikki. He began to count the days before his dad would return to the farm and take him back to Reykjavik—and another year of school.

This had certainly been a summer full of adventure. Rikki's horizon had expanded far beyond what he could possibly have imagined, to include tales of elves and trolls, as well as knowledge about the spiritual dimension. Being a soul that can never die, a soul that has lived many lives, and a soul that exists simultaneously in the spiritual dimension and on Earth, made intuitive sense. And, looking at life as a temporary journey into a physical dimension for the purpose of learning something specific about oneself made a lot of sense as well.

For Rikki, a sense of stillness and a spiritual certainty began to descend, and his life began to come into perspective for the first time. He noticed that his stammer had become more manageable and his confidence had begun to grow after he had met with Old Soul at Heather Hill. Paradoxically, the experience of accepting that he had chosen to have the stammer brought forth an inward stillness and an acceptance that to struggle in life could make him stronger.

Rikki also realized how his dyslexia had set him apart. He had been placed into the Ó class of students at the age of seven and remained there until age twelve. His school only had four categories of classes: an A class, a B class, and a C class, followed by an Ó class. Rikki often wondered what had happened to the D class, or the *E* class, etc.? Why were there no classes below the letter *C* of the alphabet until, suddenly, there was the *Ó* class? Thank God, there were no *X*, *Y*, or *Z* classes. That would have been a worse place to be!

Being in the *Ó* class, however, was okay for Rikki. During these years, he gradually began to socialize more with his classmates, as well as with students from the other classes, and he made some good friends. And now, reflecting on what Old Soul had said about life being a journey gave him the freedom not to rush or to be overcome with worry. He knew that everything would ultimately be just fine, and he began to find peace of mind and to focus on his studies and buckle down with his homework. As the months rolled by from fall to winter and to spring, he noticed that his stammer almost disappeared. His dyslexia became more manageable, and his reading ability increased. He was less fearful; he felt less different and less alone.

Chapter 3

The Farm, Holar

RIKKI DID NOT RETURN to Lakjamot the following summer, much to his father's and uncle's disappointment, as his mother still bristled at the idea the brothers had concocted to trade Rikki for one of Siggi's daughters. She also hoped that a different farm would bring some new challenges to Rikki.

So, in early spring, arrangements were made for Rikki to spend the summer at a farm in the south of Iceland, called Holar. The routine at this farm was similar to what he had become accustomed to at his uncle's farm in the north of Iceland. There were horses and sheep, as well as cows that he fetched in the mornings and herded again off to pasture, following milking. Rikki spent an unremarkable summer season on this farm when he was thirteen, but when Rikki turned fourteen, the farmer passed away from cancer. He was survived by his wife and a son, Fredrick, who was eighteen at the time and took over the running of the farm. The following summer, Rikki became quite active in supporting the young farmer. There was much to do and many chores, some of which included milking the cows by hand, although milking machines had by then taken foothold on some nearby farms. Rikki also spent many hours driving the tractor through fields around and around, acre after acre, turning hay while belting out songs, such as this one by Cliff Richards:

> "Lucky lips are always kissing
> lucky lips are never blue.
> Lucky lips will always find a pair of lips so true.
> Don't need a four-leaf clover,
> rabbit's foot or a good look charm,
> With lucky lips you'll always have
> A baby in your arms."[1] [35]

At the age of twelve, Rikki had discovered that he could sing without a hint of a stammer. This was liberating. His best friend,

---

[35]   Cliff Richard. *Lucky Lips*. Recorded in the UK, 1963. Written by Jerry Lieber & Mike Stoller.

Thor, played the guitar, and they began to practice singing Beatles songs as well as other popular music. They spent untold hours belting out songs and harmonizing together, an activity that led quickly to the establishment of a band with Rikki as the lead singer, and the following spring they began to play at school dances. This hobby continued for a couple of years, until Rikki was in his fourteenth year.

Fredrick soon fell in love with a woman by the name of Anna, whom he met at a nearby nursery. They were married a couple of years later. But their marital bliss came to an abrupt end shortly afterward, when a dreadful event occurred. Following a normal pregnancy, their firstborn developed an obscure illness a few weeks following his birth that left him paralyzed and severely mentally challenged. A couple of years later, and after much deliberation and advice from doctors who had been unable to diagnose the cause of the child's illness, Fredrick and his wife took the risk of having another child. They had a second son and were tremendously relieved that he remained perfectly healthy following his birth and he developed normally. They then felt safe in having a third child, assuming that their firstborn must have caught a stray virus or that some obscure genetic sequencing must have gone awry and caused the illness. Their third child was also a boy. This time, however, luck was not on their side, and, a few weeks after his birth, the exact same illness that befell their firstborn robbed this infant of his health as well.

Fredrick and Anna were devastated, and if not for the help and support of their community and the spiritual support they received from their church, they might not have coped. Rikki, recollecting what Old Soul had said a few years earlier about himself having chosen to stammer and having chosen his dyslexia, wondered if the souls of these boys had also chosen their fate prior to birth, and if the farmer and his wife had agreed to take on this emotional and physical burden for their own spiritual development. If that was the case, then they had certainly stepped up to the plate, as they never wavered in their love and care for the two boys—a triumph of their human spirit. This was most definitely a topic Rikki wanted to discuss with Old Soul, whenever they'd have an opportunity to meet again.

Similarly, a dreadful fate befell Fredrick's half-brother and his wife, who lived in a nearby town a few miles away. A dump truck backed up and unloaded a ton of sand onto their three-year old boy, who was playing behind the truck, causing him to suffocate from the weight of the sand. This, of course, was another topic that Rikki intended to discuss with Old Soul. Then there was a sixteen-year old friend of Rikki's, who died in a car accident. He was a passenger, when his friend, who was driving, lost control of the vehicle on a gravel road one night on the way home from a country dance. A similar fate befell one of Rikki's classmates, on whom he had a secret crush, who, also on his way home from a country dance, was pierced through the head by a metal rod that extended from the back of a lorry. He died instantly. The driver of the vehicle, also a dear friend of Rikki, and the fastest runner in school, was permanently paralyzed from the waist down. And a final story—tragedy also struck the drummer of his high-school band. He was thirteen at the time and passed out on his back with his head wedged between two tufts of moss. He had become intoxicated after drinking excessively with his friends while out camping. He vomited into his mouth and suffocated. Rikki struggled to understand these tragedies. Were they all fated? Was this God's work? Rikki resolved to get some answers to these questions from Old Soul when they next met.

Another interesting event had begun to occur. His mother had had a pregnancy, prior to Rikki's sister's birth a few years earlier. But, due to complications with her health at the time, she opted for an abortion late into that pregnancy. The child was a boy, and he grew up within the spiritual dimension.[36] He, however, longed for life on Earth and would often visit Rikki, appearing at the foot of his bed as he was about to fall asleep, as he wished to spend some time with him in other dimensions while his body slept. This was not

---

[36] For a similar account, see Todd Burpo. *Heaven Is For Real*. Nashville: Thomas Nelson, 2010.

bothersome for Rikki, but he planned also to ask Old Soul about this, as his 'spirit brother' did not appear to be like a typical ghost.

Love and Sex

A few years had passed since Rikki began to spend his summers at the farm Holar, and he was sweet sixteen. His social life was active; he was well liked and he had numerous friends. He had romantic attractions, as did his friends. Unlike his friends, however, all of the crushes Rikki experienced were for other boys. In fact, when he thought about it, as far back has he could remember, he had never been sexually attracted to the opposite sex. He had experimented with sex on numerous occasions with boys and girls prior to puberty, but following puberty, these activities became centered on males. At the time, he rationalized that the reason for this preference must have to do with his worry that a girl might become pregnant. It took a few years, however, for him to realize that he had, in fact, never been sexually attracted to girls. This self-revelation came as a shock to Rikki, and accepting it was difficult. He understood that longing romantically for another guy was not considered "cool" in his circle of friends.

So, to compensate, Rikki took to wrestling in fun with some of his more attractive mates. This provided an opportunity for intimate contact, a roll in the grass, and to pin his friends down in a variety of positions, while enjoying the sensation of their hot and throbbing bodies as they wrestled for release. For Rikki, this was the closest socially acceptable physical contact that was possible with other young men, and, while it was simply a wrestling match for his friends, for Rikki it was also a titillating forbidden sexual experience. Wrestling became less frequent by the age of sixteen, though, and was more often replaced by clandestine opportunities for mutual masturbation. These were erotic and enjoyable times, but empty in terms of romance, as all of his friends were ostensibly heterosexual.

Rikki dated a couple of girls for short periods of time, feeling that it was a social obligation, but he never felt any urges or sexual attraction for them. He knew of no other boys who were like him, and, as the years passed, he began to think that he was the only one on the planet who was attracted to the same sex. A profound sense of isolation began to descend during his late teenage years. He began to suffer loneliness for love he had never known. Would he ever experience being loved by a man? Unlike his heterosexual friends, whose love adventures were openly embraced and discussed endlessly, his romantic affections became secrets; not because he was teased or ostracized, but because he knew of no one who seemed to share the same romantic desires.

Rikki felt that there wasn't much he could do about it, other than to adapt and to camouflage this aspect of himself—and to keep his feelings hidden. This decision, however, had the effect of not only squelching his expression of romantic affections but it also, unbeknownst to himself at the time, began to decrease his ability to experience loving affection in general. He became less moved emotionally. He was less able to experience and less able to express intimate emotions, and also less able to empathize with painful emotions felt by others. In effect, he became hardened; not in a tough-guy sort of way, but rather in an emotionally numb sort of way.

As he thought about it, Rikki decided that he wanted to hear Old Soul's thoughts on the issue of his sexual orientation now more than ever.

The following year, at the age of seventeen, Rikki resolved to visit Old Soul again. Five years had passed since they had last met, and he had a lot of questions about life that needed answers. After he had returned home to the city, in preparation for another school year, Rikki decided to go for a short visit to his uncle's farm up north, at Lakjamot. It was early October and an exciting time at the farm. The hundreds of horses that belonged to all the farms in the district were being herded off the highlands and back to the farms in the valley. The farm was bustling with activity, but Rikki managed to find time to ride his horse, Trust, who was now getting on in years, out to Heather Hill for a visit with Old Soul. As before,

Rikki made his way up onto the rock, walked in circles—thrice clockwise and thrice anti-clockwise—before standing still and facing Heather Hill while thinking a loving thought of his horse, Trust. Time stood still. Heather Hill opened and Old Soul came to the door and welcomed him warmly before leading him into his private study, as he had done on their first visit.

This time, Rikki had prepared a long list of questions, which included questions about life and death and the reasons for tragedies, including the death of his friends and the illness of the two boys at Holar that had left them mentally delayed and paralyzed. He was interested in hearing what Old Soul had to say about his spirit brother, who was growing up in the spiritual dimension. Last but not least, he wanted advice about his sexual orientation.

Old Soul seemed to know what questions Rikki wanted to ask of him and said, "You have prepared a number of important questions for me, but before I can give you the answers to these questions I'll need to provide you with some background information about the nature of your existence within the physical world."

Rikki, remembering how time had stood still during their last meeting, said jokingly, "This will not take a lot of time, will it?"

Old Soul, with a smile, responded, "No, you are at this moment outside the dimension of time, but I will tell you more about that in a few minutes, so to speak!"

Rikki smiled and relaxed the best he could, seated on the same stool he had sat on during their first meeting. When he looked around, he seemed to have a view of the entire spiritual universe, despite being in the confines of Old Soul's study. It seemed a little odd to him that he could sit in Old Soul's study, yet see an entire universe. But this is what it was, and it was breathtaking.

As before, there were spirits in the form of colorful orbs meandering about. Rikki knew that Old Soul was a spirit-orb too, although appearing to Rikki in human form. But he seemed genderless, which puzzled Rikki. So he decided to ask Old Soul about this before they continued.

Rikki, speaking hesitantly, queried, "I beg your pardon. I hope you don't mind me asking you this. You look human, but I can't figure out if you are male or female."

Old Soul chuckled and replied, "I am neither, but I can be either. The assignment of gender only occurs once the soul has decided to have a lifetime on Earth. The gender of the fetus is determined during gestation. And, since you need the two genders on Earth to procreate and sustain the species, we normally choose to make the body either male or female. But here in the spiritual dimension, procreation does not take place, so there is no need to be male or female."

Rikki said, "Oh, okay."

Old Soul continued, "However, since I know you will find it easier to take the advice I have to give you from a male figure, please feel free to think of me and to refer to me in the male pronoun."

Rikki replied, "Okay, I will."

Old Soul was dressed in a white robe, and a light blue aura seemed to emanate around him. He had a large medallion hanging on a golden cord around his neck. The medallion appeared to be some sort of a mirror, because every time Rikki attempted to look at, it was as if his own entire life until then was reflected back onto him.

Rikki commented, "That is a nice medallion you have. When I look at it, I see my entire life until now."

Old Soul said, "Yes, most of us have one of these here in the spirit world. It helps us with our tasks as fylgjur."

As Rikki looked at Old Soul, he realized that, although he knew Old Soul to be very old, he appeared as if in the prime of his life—even younger than his dad, Baldur. Old Soul had dirty blond hair, heavy eyebrows, and dark brown eyes.

A deep sense of kindness emanated from Old Soul as he began to speak quietly. "Now, let's get back on topic and begin with our lesson for today."

Rikki prepared himself to receive some important information.

Old Soul continued, "You do not realize how much information you need to know in order to understand fully the answers that I'd like to give you to the questions you have prepared for me today."

Rikki, with a smile, said, "Well, since I'm outside the dimension of time, I suppose the time it takes for you to explain will not be an issue."

Old Soul smiled and continued, "Before I can give you some of the answers to your questions, I'll have to explain a few concepts. First I'll need to tell you a little bit about how the universe is created, and next, how you create your reality within it."

Rikki agreed, "That sounds like a lot of information."

Old Soul said, "Yes it is. But your questions have to do with important issues concerning life and death, and unless you have a basic understanding of these concepts, you will not be able to understand the reason and logic to my answers."

Rikki said, "Well, I'm ready. Let's start. Do you think it is possible for me to understand how the universe is created?"

Old Soul answered, "Yes, in a limited way."

The Basic Universe

"Let me try to explain how the universe is put together by way of an analogy. Imagine that 'All That Is,' or God, is a huge conscious organism. Everything that exists is housed within this organism, and there is, therefore, consciousness in everything that exists. This organism is self-sustaining, and it creates within it a type of 'action' or 'happening,' through God's intent. This action activates minute particles called 'consciousness units' that are the basic building blocks within the organism."

> All speech, action and behavior are fluctuations of consciousness. All life emerges from, and is sustained in, consciousness. The whole universe is the expression of consciousness. The reality of the universe is one unbounded ocean of consciousness in motion.
>
> *- Maharishi Mahesh Yogi*

Rikki said, "Okay, I remember you mentioning something about consciousness units in the homework you gave me following our first meeting."

Old Soul said, "Yes. And today I will elaborate on the concepts I told you about then."

Old Soul, continued, "When action activates these consciousness units, they begin to combine in accordance with their specialization. So, for example, when the universe was created, a specialized group of consciousness units coalesced to form dimensions. They created the physical dimension and the spiritual dimension. Yet other consciousness units created dimensions nested within these dimensions, such as the dimensions of space and time within your physical dimension."

There is consciousness in everything that exists.

Rikki said thoughtfully, "Okay, I'm following you."

Old Soul continued, "Within the physical dimension, there were also consciousness units that coalesced to form a general platform or a 'canvas.' All structures that appear within the physical dimension are formed out of this canvas. From your perspective, this canvas is, of course, invisible; it is in the background. You only see the structures it creates as they emerge into the physical universe. Examples include the galaxies, the stars, your solar system and the planets, as well as everything on Earth, the stratosphere, the biosphere, and all physical structures on the planet, including the mountains, water, flora, and fauna.

"A similar canvas exists within the spiritual dimension. But the structures that are created there are non-physical, or mental. There is also a huge qualitative difference between the consciousness that comprises the canvas within the spiritual dimension and that which makes up the canvas in the physical universe. The consciousness in the spiritual dimension is much more sophisticated. It is out of this canvas that the over-souls emerge—these are discrete orbs of self-aware, highly intelligent bundles of consciousness."

Rikki interjected, "Okay, I think I am following you, so far."

Old Soul continued. "An important feature for you to understand, is that all the structures that form, or evolve, out of the canvas do so in a circular fashion—they evolve and then disintegrate back into their basic elements and then combine again, only to disintegrate once more. These circular patterns are universal, and they take place both within the spiritual universe and within the physical universe."

Rikki asked, "What type of circular patterns are you talking about?"

Old Soul replied, "Here is an example. Within the spiritual universe, at the highest level, a newborn over-soul separates from All That Is, or from God[37]. The over-soul has no memory of its past, and it is

---

[37]   Michael Newton. *Destiny Of Souls*. St. Paul: Llewellyn Publications, 2000.

intrinsically motivated and curious to learn. As it learns, it evolves and ascends slowly through the stages of spiritual awareness within the spiritual universe, until it eventually rejoins All That Is. During this process of evolving, it projects souls into numerous mental and physical dimensions, in order to seek experiences from which it will learn. One of these physical dimensions contains your solar system and the planet Earth."

Rikki nodded. "Okay, I see."

Old Soul continued, "This circular pattern within the physical dimension is similar, but it is aided by a process which I will refer to as the 'unfolding harmony.' The unfolding harmony is an ongoing process that strings events out within the dimension of time. It is responsible for coordinating the circular universal patterns that take place within your physical dimension, as it brings about the emergence of structures that are created by the canvas and strings them out in perfect harmony and in perfect synchrony. Were it not for the unfolding harmony and the time dimension, everything would appear to happen at once within your physical dimension.

"The structures that the unfolding harmony brings about come in and out of existence in circular patters as they form, or grow, out of basic elements and then disintegrate back into their basic constituents, only to form again."

Rikki said, "Okay, I think I understand. An invisible canvas creates the structures, and the unfolding harmony strings them out within the dimension of time in my physical world."

Old Soul said, "Correct. Again, as an example, you observe the pattern whereby rocks are formed and then erode within a time scale spanning millions of years. Similarly, but on shorter time scales, more complex structures evolve, such as life forms that also have circular patterns of evolvement, commonly referred to as a lifespan. These life forms become increasingly complex as they evolve from flora to fauna, to include mammals and humans."

Rikki said, "Okay. I understand."

Old Soul continued, "Now, as I said earlier, the type of consciousness that is contained within the canvas in the physical dimension is considerably less sophisticated, compared with the consciousness within the spiritual dimension. The difference between these two types of consciousness is so vast that it renders them fundamentally different, in that animals and humans created out of the canvas that forms the physical dimension are not sufficiently complex to be sentient or self-aware, as are the over-souls that emerge from the canvas in the spiritual dimension."

Rikki asked, "Are you saying that the human being is not sentient or self-aware?"

Old Soul said, "The human being would remain an animal at this stage, were it not for what I'm now about to explain."

Rikki said, "Oh, okay."

Old Soul, now gesturing with his hands, went on, "This is how this all ties together. I hinted at this before, in the homework I gave you after our last meeting. Over-souls, in availing themselves of an opportunity to learn about themselves in the physical world, project their souls into the consciousness of the human fetus during the time of gestation. As this happens, the human animal becomes sentient or self-aware."

Rikki, with a smile, said, "Okay, I see. Well, that's a relief!" He paused, thinking. "That's incredible!"

Old Soul said, "Well, yes, that is what some people refer to as a miracle. That is how we, as souls, enter into the physical world when we become incarnate."

Rikki said, "I like that."

Old Soul continued, "Yes, and fortunately there is no shortage of over-souls eager to project souls into the physical dimension for the experience of a lifetime on Earth. So, consequently, all human beings are sentient.

Rikki said, "Okay, I understand. I have a quick question, though. You once said that I've had dozens of past lives. Am I the same soul that reincarnates again and again?"

Old Soul replied, "You, that is, your over-soul, has projected many souls onto Earth over the past few hundred years, but it is never the exact same soul that reincarnates. You prepare a different soul for every incarnation. Every soul comprises numerous qualities contained within your over-soul, including experiences obtained from your over-soul's souls past incarnations. Unresolved issues from previous incarnations are often also included in the new soul, in order to give the new soul an opportunity to do further work on those issues. An example that pertains to you was your fear of water. This fear originated a long time ago, but remained unresolved. So you decided to bring it around in this current incarnation, and it has now been resolved. Specific talents are also brought forward occasionally for further development."

Rikki queried, "You mean like with a child prodigy?"

Old Soul said, "Yes. The over-soul may include a specific ability that was developed in a past life, or over successive past lives, in order to work with it further.

"Every incarnation commences with a newborn body and a new soul—or more accurately, a newly revised soul. In preparing the new soul, you make prominent certain personality characteristics that you anticipate will enable you to meet the demands of the fated events you've set in place, so that you will achieve insights about your inner nature. As the over-soul learns about itself over successive incarnation cycles, it matures and evolves spiritually. You should also know that every soul your over-soul has ever projected onto Earth retains its identity following the incarnation, and you can have access to its memories and emotional experiences after your lifetime is completed and you have returned to the spiritual dimension. If you wish, you may also have access to those past lives during your current incarnation, during a past-life regression."

Rikki responded, "Okay. That makes it clear.

"There is another point I'd like to understand a little better before we continue, if I may?"

Old Soul replied, "Of course. What's on your mind?"

Rikki asked, "You mentioned in the homework you gave me, following our first meeting, that life on Earth is mainly about 'inner learning' that takes place when we create emotional experiences. What about everything else that occurs during a lifetime that is not specifically about emotions? Isn't that important too"?

Old Soul hesitated, and replied, "That's a good question. It will take us off topic for a few minutes, but I think it would be helpful if I provided a brief answer, before we proceed.

"The common view on Earth is that life is mainly about achievements and successes through activities, such as work, but that is not the case. As I said before, the main reason for your incarnation is to experience emotions that do not occur here in the spiritual dimension, and to benefit from the inner learning that takes place when you have them. All other events during your lifetime are primarily vehicles to having these emotional experiences."

Rikki, elaborating on his question, asked, "Do you mean that everything else people do in life, such as studying, striving towards having a career, working, making money, and so on, is not important?"

Old Soul replied, "No, these pursuits are also essential. They offer fulfillment, purpose, and meaning throughout a person's lifetime, and I'll be telling you more about that later. More importantly, these pursuits help create the context in which emotional experiences can take place. Through these pursuits, persons find themselves in different life circumstances, in which their mental character, when paired with the uniqueness of the situation, provides the seed for a specific emotional experience to take place.

Rikki asked, thoughtfully, "Is life mainly about manufacturing emotions?"

Old Soul replied, "Yes, in essence, it is. Specialized 'consciousness units' coalesce to form a 'feeling-state' that is the basis of all emotion. Your conscious intent then causes a build-up of this feeling-state, increasing its strength. And finally, it is the combination of your conscious intent, on the one hand, your mental character, and your particular life circumstance on the other, that defines the emotion—or gives it a name. For example, if you experience an intense fear while riding in an elevator, you may, depending on your mental character, develop a 'phobia of elevators'. Similarly, a fright on a rooftop of a building, may, result in a 'fear of heights'.

"Once an emotion is generated, it often generalizes to other similar situations. For example, the person experiencing phobias of elevators and of heights may develop a fear of all enclosed spaces, and of all situations involving heights. This characteristic of generalization is especially problematic with negative emotions including, for example, fear, anxiety, jealousy, anger, depression, and guilt—because it causes them to spread, like a fog. The fog lays a blanket of haze over an entire terrain of similar circumstances, as it settles in and infuses the person, sometimes for days, weeks, and months. This same type of generalization also occurs for positive emotions, where, for example, after a joyous event, the emotions of love, joy, and happiness, bathe the person in sublime rays of sunshine—often for long periods of time. It will comfort you to know, however, that over the course of time, for all instances that involve negative and painful emotions, love (which is the basic nature of the soul) gains the upper hand, causing negative emotions to dissolve, just as when the rays of the sun, break-up the blanket of fog."

Rikki, wanting to have a better understanding of this relationship between emotions and intelligence, asked, "But, what about intelligence, and intellectual pursuits? Surely, life on Earth must rely more on intelligence than on the volatility of emotions?"

Old Soul replied, "An incarnation is not undertaken in order to advance the soul's intelligence. The over-soul's and the soul's intellectual capacity far surpass what is expressed through the human body during an incarnation. That is why (and I will talk more about this later) you should accept that every human being is equally valid. There is no difference in intelligence between the soul that has melded with a body of a person who is mentally challenged, who does not pursue an education, who is a "bum", or a garbage collector, and the souls of those individuals who are thought to be the most successful members of society, such as Nobel laureates and heads of states."

Rikki said, "I don't understand. From what I can see, there is a big difference between these individuals."

Old Soul replied, "Yes there is, but the difference is not between the intellectual capacities of their souls, but rather in the deliberate design that takes place when the soul is melding with the fetus during gestation. The soul, wishing to experience circumstances that will lead to a specific quality of emotion, chooses the cultural and demographic settings into which it will incarnate, and endows the fetus with a mental capacity, and a character, that will lead it, or limit it, to specific pursuits during the incarnation. The soul, in this way, seeks to create the optimal context for specific emotional experiences to take place.

"From the over-soul's and the soul's perspective, pursuits during an incarnation are mainly designed to bring about the conditions that offer an opportunity to experience specific types of emotion. Intellectual pursuits, and abilities that are honed during the course of a lifetime are also important, but they are secondary and not the primary objective of the soul's incarnation."

Rikki relented and said, "O.K., I see what you mean. But what happens when emotions get out of hand? Do you think there is enough intelligence on the globe to guide the human race away from self-destruction?"

Old Soul smiled and replied, "Yes, there is."

In summing up his comments, Old Soul continued, "All souls that incarnate on Earth, aside from a few spiritual guides, do so in order to learn about emotions. The ultimate challenge during an incarnation is to live your life with loving intent (which is a reflection of your soul's nature), while at the same time experiencing, and learning about, all the painful and negative emotions that take place. It is the manner in which you handle these emotions when they are intense and overwhelming, and the decisions you make during those times, that lead you to discoveries about your inner nature. Eventually, as you learn how to transcend these emotions, you evolve spiritually.

"I will tell you much more about how this inner learning takes place later on, as we continue our discussions. But, let's now get back on topic.

Rikki interjected, "O.K. thank you for clarifying these issues."

Old Soul continued, As I was saying, aside from a basic biology that influences the morphology of the human body, it is the soul that is responsible for making the human unique and self-aware. It is through the melding between the soul's consciousness and the consciousness of the human body that a sentient human being is created. The sentient human being is, in effect, a combination of two types of consciousness—he is in part sophisticated soul consciousness and in part elementary consciousness created out of specialized consciousness units contained within the canvas that creates everything within the physical universe."

Rikki said, "Okay, I understand."

Old Soul said, "So, it is the combination of the body and the soul that make the human being sentient or self-aware. The body functions both as a personal camera, through which you can experience the physical world, and also as a vehicle, which you use to move about while on the planet during your lifetime. This body equipment has some interesting qualities, and it requires regular maintenance. It's important that I describe some of this to you briefly, before we go further."

Rikki, smiling, agreed. "Okay. You describe the body as a camera and as a car."

Old Soul said, "Yes. It's a good analogy, don't you think? And you have had different cars in past lives, all of which have operated slightly differently, because no two physical bodies are exactly the same."

The Basic Physical Body

Old Soul continued, "The basic physical body has some attributes that are always the same. These attributes give the body an ability to perceive the physical world, and I'll describe them to you first. Then I'll briefly describe some of the basic needs your body must have met in order to function properly. And finally, I'll talk briefly about some of the challenges the body is faced with as you use it to maneuver about within the physical world.

"The most basic attribute of your body is its ability to detect 'physical contrast.'

"The physical body is innately drawn to contrast, as this is the foundational source through which it is able to experience the physical world. If you did not have the ability to detect contrast, you would not be able to perceive anything and, consequently, you would not have a single experience. The perception of contrast is achieved through your sensory mechanisms, and it is through them that you are able to experience your physical existence. For example: Your **eyes** have an ability to detect the contrast between frequencies of light and allow you to see a spectrum of color within a specific range of wavelengths; the **ears** have an ability to identify contrast in the wavelengths that carry sound and allow you to hear within a specific frequency range; receptors in the **skin** give you the ability to sense energy in the form of heat and allow you to experience contrast in temperature fluctuations that, in turn, aid you in maintaining a comfortable body temperature and preventing hypothermia and heat exhaustion. **Touch receptors** in your skin allow you to experience contrast by detecting differences in texture, pressure, vibration, and pain; **taste receptors** in your tongue allow you to discriminate the contrast among five different types of taste—salty, sour, bitter, sweet, and savory. **Olfactory receptors** in your nostrils detect airborne droplets and allow you to experience contrast of different types of smell."

Rikki, listening carefully, said, "Hmm, I've never really thought about it in this way."

Old Soul said, "Most people haven't."

He continued, "The combined Information that is gathered from these sensory mechanisms adds up to a kaleidoscope of experiences that enable you to perceive the physical world from numerous perspectives.

"Now, the basic needs that your body requires in order to function properly include light, gravity, sleep, rest, and nutrition. This is, of course, obvious to you, but let me nevertheless comment on these aspects very briefly.

"Your body, and indeed all life on the surface of the Earth, is sustained by light provided by the sun. Were it not for the sun, all life would cease within 8.3 minutes, which is the time it takes for light particles to travel from the sun at a speed of almost three million meters per second."

Rikki said, surprised, "Oh. That would be a quick end."

Old Soul said, "Yes, but fortunately it is something you do not have to worry about. But your body is affected by light in numerous ways; the most obvious being that you are unable to see when it's dark, so your ability to maneuver about at night is severely restricted. Sunlight also stimulates your body to produce vitamin D, which is a necessary substance for your body. It also stimulates neurochemical reactions in your brain that are important for regulating your mood. That is why, in the absence of sunlight during the winter months, some people begin to feel depressed."

Rikki commented, "I know a couple of people who always feel depressed during the dark winter months."

Old Soul said, "Yes, it's a fairly common problem. Sunlight, or a bright light, is the best cure for them."

Old Soul continued, "Gravity is another important feature that has an effect on the body.

"A gravitational force acts on all matter, causing it to be pulled down toward your planet. Your body requires this force to grow and to function properly. Were it not for gravity, you would not be able to walk about the surface of the planet or keep your body healthy through regular exercise. The gravitational force is contained within an invisible field surrounding the planet, and it dissipates and decreases in intensity as you travel away from Earth.

"Finally, sleep, rest, and nutrition are also essential for the body to function properly.

"Your body has developed circadian rhythms in its adaptation to light, where it produces a hormone that induces sleep and forces it to rest when darkness descends. The body produces a different hormone when light returns, awaking it and keeping it alert throughout the day. During sleep, your body rests and restores itself. Another convenient byproduct of sleep is that while your body sleeps, your soul can leave your body and attend to other business. The activity of the soul while your body sleeps will often be recalled in distorted forms as dreams when you awake in the morning. And lastly, your body must, of course, receive adequate nutrition at regular intervals in order for it to function."

Rikki, picking up on the topic of dreams, said, "I enjoy my travels in other dimensions while my body sleeps."

Old Soul said, "Yes, I know. You can enhance your memories of these adventures by practicing a technique called 'lucid dreaming,', but that is a topic we may discuss at a later time."

Old Soul continued, "Now that I've briefly reviewed how your body perceives its surroundings and what it needs to be maintained, let's look at a couple of physical challenges you must contend with on Earth. First we have the climate.

"The climate and seasonal weather patterns are factors that force your body to adapt to certain environmental conditions and to schedule activities while taking account of the weather and the contrast of the seasons.

"You experience the effects of the Earth rotating on its axis every twenty-four hours, and, as it rotates, daylight is affected in most regions and temperature fluctuations occur due to the absence of heat caused by sunlight. This causes stirrings in the atmosphere that affect weather patterns as well as the ocean currents, and these often restrict human activity on the planet. Also, as the Earth travels on its orbit around the sun every 365 days and tilts on its axis relative to the plane of its revolution, you observe seasonal climate changes.

"To everything there is a season, And a time to every purpose under the heaven."

- Ecclesiastes 3:1

These seasonal climate changes become more distinct as you move to areas of the planet that are further away from the equator, like here in Iceland. In the northern hemisphere, there is more sunlight in May, June, and July, because this hemisphere faces the sun at those times, whereas in November, December, and January, the southern hemisphere faces the sun and gets the sunlight, while it is dark most of the time up here. You, of course, accept this aspect of your environment, and you schedule your activities accordingly."

"There is one additional challenge which I'll mention at this time, although it relates more to your soul than to your body. It has to do with the frustrating task your soul has with maneuvering your body about on Earth within the space/time dimension."

Old Soul continued, "You may find this example a little more interesting. The dimensions of space and time appear to you to be independent of one another, but they are in fact woven together. I'll call them 'space/time.' Space/time is an aspect of the physical world that is a challenge for all souls when they become incarnate, as these dimensions do not exist in the spiritual dimension. There are many facets to this experience that we could talk about, but I will only mention a few at this time.

"For one, the adjustment a soul must make while trapped within the confines of a physical body is not easy. In the spiritual dimension you are accustomed to 'think' and then to 'be' in a new location instantly, but on Earth you have to make a telephone call or spend the 'time' it takes to move your physical body through 'space' from one location to another, in order to communicate with another person at a distance. Your 'thoughts' will, however, continue to travel instantly and they will be picked up by whomever you send them to, provided that that person is telepathically receptive, but, unlike in the spiritual dimension, this is not a reliable way to communicate on Earth. Contending with space/time is the single most frustrating experience your soul will have throughout your incarnation, and I will tell you much more about this later on."

Rikki said, "Now I realize why I'm so often frustrated when I can't get to where I want to go fast enough."

Old Soul said, "Yes. As you know, there are essentially two aspects of time that you now experience. On the one hand you have 'clock' time (derived as a function of one rotation of the Earth around its own axis, divided into segments of twenty-four hours; each hour divided into sixty minutes, and each minute into sixty seconds), and on the other, you have your personal experience of the passage of time. As you know, you frequently experience these delineations of time to be at odds with one another. However, if you want to operate effectively on Earth, you must learn to schedule your life according to clock time, as you will not thrive unless you are able, for example, to be on clock time for appointments, for work, or to catch a bus or a train, etc. The difficulty is that your personal experience of the passage of time is often at odds with clock time. Sometimes, you will experience it to be faster and at other times slower, relative to clock time. For example, in reply to your comment—when you are in a hurry to get somewhere, your personal experience of the passage of time seems to be slow and you feel as if it takes forever to arrive at your destination. Whereas if you are absorbed in some

> How long a minute is, depends on which side of the bathroom door you're on.
>
> - *Zall's law.*

activity, such as doing your homework, your personal experience of the passage of time is faster, relative to clock time."

Rikki nodded. "Yes, I understand."

Old Soul said, "Now I have described in elementary terms how the universe is created and how it functions. I also described how sentient human beings are created and the basic aspects of the physical body, including some of the restrictions imposed on it by the climate and by space/time.

"Now let me attempt to explain to you how you create your reality by using this human body we just described."

You Create Your Reality

Old Soul continued, "Remember, I said that structures are created within the canvas, and the unfolding harmony coordinates the appearance of these structures within the physical dimension."

You create your reality.

Rikki said, "Yes. Everything I see in my physical world is created out of the background canvas."

Old Soul said, "Yes, but you only see what you want to see or what you expect to see."

Rikki asked, "Really? How does that happen?"

Old Soul said, "There are fluid interactions that occur between yourself and your environment that determine how you perceive what is around you. There is not one single interaction that is responsible for how you perceive your world, but many that work in unison, fluidly, all influencing one other. I'll attempt to explain some of these processes to you."

Rikki said, "Okay, I'm listening."

Old Soul said, "First, I'd like you to imagine that your body is a handheld movie camera. As you walk around, you record everything you point the camera's lens at. On the one hand, you know that there are physical structures all around you, but on the other hand, you only make a copy of what hits the lens."

Rikki said, "Okay, so I only see what I look at, but I know, at the same time, that there is other stuff around."

Old Soul continued, "Yes, and what you look at is interpreted on at least two levels. When you point your lens at something, you make a copy. But there is more to this copy than meets the eye. You don't appreciate how important this is until you begin to compare your copies with the copies of a friend who has, for example, walked with you down the same street and pointed his lens on exactly the same structures. What you discover is that you agree on what you have seen in terms of surface detail. You might say that your observations are objective, on this level of analysis. However, when you look at the detail, you quickly discover that his interpretations of what he saw are entirely differently from yours, almost to the extent that it would appear that the two of you had walked down entirely different streets. Objectively, you walked down the same street, but subjectively the copy you made of the experience is entirely different from his. When you look below the surface agreements, you discover that your subjective experience is, in fact, unique."

Rikki said, "I see. I didn't realize the extent of this."

Old Soul said, "Yes. This is an example of where you both have created separate realities. You have discovered that the realities you created are similar on the surface, but unique when analyzed more closely, from a subjective perspective."

Rikki, feeling that a little levity was in order after this heavy material, recalled a passage he had read in an article a few days earlier about Zen Buddhism and said, teasingly, "So, answer this question for me. What is the sight of a tree falling in the forest, when no one is looking? And what is the sound of one hand clapping?"

Old Soul laughed. "This is an age-old tease, questioning the unfathomable. For our purposes here today, which are purely practical, my answer to you would be: Unless you make a visual copy, or an auditory copy of the event, then it did not happen. In terms of your question, if you did not see the tree falling and if you did not hear the clap of one hand, then it did not happen."

Rikki asked, "What if someone told me about something I did not see or hear, or if I read about it. Did it happen?"

Old Soul said, "You have to judge the likelihood as to whether it occurred. All you have is a copy of the experience created by having heard about it or read about it. That is your reality. And as I said earlier, the more closely you scrutinize your experience of having read something or heard something and then compare it to someone else's experience, the more at variance you discover your experience to be. Your reality is unique. You create it for yourself."

> Reality is unset Jell-O. There's a big indeterminate sludge out there that's our potential life. And we, by our very act of involvement, our act of noticing, our observation, we get that Jell-O to set. So we're intrinsic to the whole process of reality. Our involvement creates reality.
>
> *- Lynne McTaggart*

Rikki said, grinning, "Okay, I see. And what if I never heard about it happening and I never knew it happened. Did it then happen?"

Old Soul said, smiling, "You don't give up do you? There are, of course, events that happen that *you know can happen*, but you do not know if they happened. Events which you may later find out either happened or did not happen—or may have happened. There are also events that happen that *you do not know could happen*, but they do happen, and you discover later that they either did happen or that they did not happen—or that you can never know if they happened at all."

Rikki and Old Soul were both grinning widely by now, as Rikki wrestled with this verbal tease about the unfathomable. Old Soul said, "In the end, whatever the copy you have of an event in your mind, that is the reality you have created for yourself.

"On a greater level, there is no right or wrong answer when you debate the unfathomable. There is only one answer: the answer that works for you. Now, let me continue where we left off."

Rikki, having enjoyed this short digression, said, "Okay."

Old Soul continued, "The reason you create your own unique reality has to do with your history. All the memories of all the experiences your over-soul has ever had during the course of past lives, including experiences within non-physical universes, have made you unique. These past influences, together with the experiences you have had in this current lifetime, make you who you are. And it is because of this that your subjective observations do not match anyone else's."

Old Soul continued, "There is more to this than first meets the eye, because these past experiences also create a type of trance within you. A trance is when your attention is drawn to something you are doing or to something that is happening, to the extent that you notice less of what is going on around you. In fact, the truth is, everyone is always in a trance.[38]"

Rikki said, "Oh, really?"

Old Soul said, "Yes, and this trance explains, in part, why your subjective reality is unique. You are in a trance, for example, when you are thinking about something, reading a book, or talking to someone. During these times, your attention is focused and you notice less what is going on around you. These are trance states; they create focus and orient you with intent."

Old Soul continued, "Now, when you add emotion to the trance, you become even more focused. And the more intense the emotion, the deeper the trance becomes."

---

[38] For more information on trance states, see Adam Crabtree, *Trance Zero: Breaking The Spell Of Conformity. Toronto*: Somerville House, 1997.

Rikki said, "Wow. I see."

Old Soul said, "This can become a problem for people who experience intense emotions, for example when they are depressed or anxious, because the trance makes it difficult for them to snap out of it. But I'll tell you more about that later. For now, all I want you to realize is that the combination of your uniqueness, the trance state, and the emotion, all influence how you experience your subjective reality, or indeed, how you create it for yourself."

> In reality, we can't really say that we're seeing the world objectively as it is. There is no completely objective appraisal of anything, because our appraisal of everything has to do with our previous experiences and our emotions. Everything has an emotional weighting to it.
>
> *- Daniel Monti, M.D.*

Rikki said, "Okay."

Old Soul said, "But there is more to the fluid interactions of the processes that produce your subjective reality. Your thoughts, your intent, and your will play a very significant role as well."

Rikki asked, "In what way does that happen?"

Old Soul said, "Let me first tell you about a discovery that has been made in physics. It has to do with a particular type of problem that occurs when you attempt to look at exceedingly small physical units. At that end of the spectrum, in other words, at the quantum level and beyond, physicists have discovered that their own conscious intent literally creates what they expect to see. They have actually discovered that they, themselves, create the outcome of their own experiments. Or, in other words, at the quantum level, they create their reality.[39]"

---

[39] Joseph Norwood. *Physics, Consciousness and the Nature of Existence.* Joseph Norwood, 2002.

Rikki said, "Oh, scientific proof. That is fantastic. Is that a problem for science?"

Old Soul said, "No, not normally, since nearly all research manipulates elements that are larger in size then the quantum. But it is important for you to know what happens here, because it has to do with how you create your own experiences. The reason for this lies in the fact that you are, in part, made out of the same type of consciousness units that comprise the canvas you are looking at."

Rikki asked, "Oh. What do you mean?"

Old Soul replied, "The problem is that the part of you that is constructed from the elementary consciousness of the canvas is the same type of consciousness you are attempting to study. In some ways, you are looking in a mirror, studying yourself at the quantum level. At the level of the quantum, your own consciousness begins to have a direct effect on the consciousness units within the canvas. Your conscious *intent* influences the consciousness of the canvas, and, in effect, pulls at the fabric of the canvas and creates out of it what you expect to see. In this way, at the quantum level, scientists have proven that you create your reality. Any scientific study of physical phenomena beyond this level is therefore futile, as this is the gateway through which thoughts become physical."

Rikki said, "I see."

Old Soul continued, "What I want to point out is that this is the gateway through which mental images materialize into your physical universe. It is through similar gateways that your own conscious intent—your thoughts, aspirations, and dreams—emerge and become reality in your physical world.[40] So, once again, this is also how you create your own reality."

---

[40] For further reading on this subject, please see: Norman Friedman, *Bridging Science and Spirit*. St. Louis: Living Lake Books, 1990. Also, Rosenblum & Kuttner, *The Quantum Enigma: Physics Encounters Consciousness*. New York: Oxford Univeristy, 2006.

Rikki wondered aloud, "So it is true? My hopes and dreams can come true?"

Old Soul leaned forward in his easy chair and continued, "Yes, they can. But there is more to how you create your reality. There is also fate."

Rikki asked, "I suppose that complicates the picture even further?"

Old Soul said, "Well, it does! There is a fluid interaction between your thoughts and intentions when you set yourself a long-term goal and your fate. Remember, you exist simultaneously outside the dimension of time, and it is the unfolding harmony that strings events out within the time dimension. Your physical body is stuck in the time dimension, but your thoughts are not. Now, in order for an event pertaining to yourself to occur, you have to have had that thought first. The more energy you put into your thought, or the stronger your conscious intent, the more likely it is that that thought will eventually materialize. That is why it is important for you to set long-term goals if there is something in particular you'd like to achieve. When you set yourself a long-term goal, you envisage a goalpost; you create a destination that provides a decisive direction for you to work toward and on which to focus your thoughts. And, over time, your intent to achieve this goal influences the consciousness units within the background canvas—which eventually bring about the materialization of your wish."

Rikki said, "I see. But I know you are going to tell me it's not that simple. Because if it were, everyone would get what they wished for."

Old Soul said, "Absolutely right. There is more to this process by which you achieve your goals in life. It's a little more complicated."

Rikki, smiling continued, "Why, why must that be?"

Old Soul responded, "Well, I'll tell you a little bit more about it. It has to do with the fluid interaction between your fate and your free will. As I mentioned in the homework I gave you following our last session, you made some rough plans prior to your birth about what you wished would happen in this lifetime—the persons you would meet who will play a major role in your life, the places in which you would spend much of your life, and the types of challenges you would encounter. These are fated events that are very likely to occur.

"You also set for yourself certain goals that you hoped to achieve in this lifetime, along with certain fated events that are associated with these goals. Your 'inner identity' is aware of this setup. But this setup is not fixed, and you can modify it as you go through life, because you have free will."

Rikki asked, "Are you saying that I have control to change my destiny?"

Old Soul answered, "Yes. With every long-term goal you set, you also set in place certain fated events that will occur as you proceed toward that destination or goal. This relationship is fluid. In other words, you have free will to change your mind and to set new goalposts whenever you wish, but as you do so, you unconsciously also set new fated events in your path. There is always an interaction between the long-term goals you set and fated events."

Rikki asked, "Why is there a relationship between my long-term goals and my fate?"

Old Soul said, "Remember, you exist simultaneously in the spiritual dimension, and from that vantage point, you are able to see your probable future within the physical dimension. Your life on Earth is a finite journey, during which you have set yourself certain objectives. Your objectives always include a lot more than meets the eye, or a specific long-term goal that you may set for yourself. So, when you decide upon a long-term goal in the present, you are, in the same moment, able to view the future consequences of that goal. And as you do that, you—still in the same moment—place specific fated events into your future path that will appear as the unfolding harmony of events brings them about. This is all to allow you to give yourself the opportunity to meet as many of your objectives during your lifetime as is possible."

Rikki mused, "Okay. It seems from what you are saying that I have control over my life and that I direct the course of my life at every moment, through my free will. And at the same time, I am also vigilant about meeting my spiritual objectives, and I therefore place fated events in my path."

Old Soul said, "Yes. The center of all change is always in the moment—in your current moment. You have free will, you make decisions, and you set goals. Remember, there is a back and forth relationship between your existence within the spiritual dimension and the physical dimension. And, as a significant part of you exists outside the time dimension, you have the advantage of knowing the consequences of your actions in advance. Your outer ego, of course, is not conscious of this, but your soul and over-soul certainly are."

Rikki said, "I see."

Old Soul continued, "So this is another way in which you create your reality—through your free will and freedom to set long-term goals as well as fated events."

Rikki smiled. "Now I'm beginning to see the big picture."

You create your reality through fluid relationships that occur between: the uniqueness of your soul, trance states, emotions, long-term goals, intent, fate, and free will.

Old Soul paused in his delivery and said, "We have covered a lot of material today, and I'd like to give you a break before we proceed. You need a little time to digest what I've told you about today."

Rikki agreed. "Yes, that sounds like a good idea. It must be getting late."

Old Soul, smiling, said, "No, not really! But I'd like you to digest some of this information for a few of your Earth hours before we proceed. Are you able to come out for another visit tomorrow?"

Rikki said, "Yes, that won't be a problem."

Old Soul stood up and walked with Rikki to a door. As he opened the door, Rikki could see through it, into the physical world, as if he was looking through a porthole. As he stepped forward, a force seemed to pull him forward, and he instantly found himself standing outside Heather Hill. And, as with his first visit to see Old Soul, time had stood still. His horse, Trust, was exactly in the same position. Not even a minute movement had occurred—not so much as a shake of his head, a blowing of his nostrils, a swat of his tail, or even a blink of an eye. Rikki understood better, this time around, how he had stepped into the spiritual dimension and out of the temporal dimension.

As Rikki rode back to the farm, he could see a herd of at least two hundred horses trotting along a gravel road in the distance east of him, churning up a cloud of dust as they headed down into Shrub Valley from the highlands. As he looked at the herd of horses making their way toward him, he was reminded of what Old Soul had said about space and time—the distance between himself and the herd and the time it took for them to approach. For the first time, he was able to formulate these dimensions more clearly in his mind. He was hyper-aware of his senses. Everything around seemed more vibrant and intense as he appreciated the contrast of the colors in the sky, the sounds of nature, the aroma from the heather as it wafted across his face, and the sweet musky smell of his horse as he carefully made his way across the patches of marsh and trotted along old sheep paths alongside small gravel mounds leading back to the farm.

There was a lot to consider from what he had learned today, and too much to think about all at once. A few things stood out in his mind as he made his way back to the farm.

As Rikki continued to ride, he engaged in an internal dialogue with himself: *It was interesting to learn that beyond everyone's perception, there is a conscious canvas that acts as a platform for literally everything that emerges into the physical world, not only for physical structures but for events as well. But we can never perceive this canvas accurately because of the fluid interaction that occurs between the consciousness of the platform and our own consciousness when we look at it.*

Rikki continued to make attempts at articulating these concepts. *Every person produces a subjective impression of what he is looking at, that aligns itself with what he expects to see. So each person literally creates a unique copy of what he sees with his eyes. Maybe it's like being partially blind; you see a basic outline and then you make up the detail.*

Rikki thought further: *This isn't only true for what we see with our eyes, it's also the same for events. Every person produces a subjective impression of an event that aligns itself with his expectations. So each person literally creates a unique copy of every event he experiences. Maybe it's like having an impression; you have a vague sense of something, and then you make up the detail.*

And his thoughts continued: *This process of creating is sufficiently consistent between individuals that they can talk about something being objective, but when you ask them to analyze their observations more deeply, you discover vast subjective differences, because everyone is unique. And there is more. We are perpetually in a trance that ebbs and flows, depending on the intensity of our emotions. And we create our emotions by placing fated events in our paths that provide the opportunities for us to create these emotions, so that we can learn about our inner nature.*

As Rikki arrived at the farm, the herd of horses, mostly mares and their foals, came trotting along the old road, outside the turf and stone wall that formed a partial fence around the lawn on the west side of the farm. The horses were tired, sweating, and snorting, as they made their way toward the parcel of land that had been fenced in; this was where they'd spend the night. It was a truly beautiful sight. The sun was beginning to set by the time the horses arrived, and evening milking was almost finished. Siggi had been on a three-day trek to gather the horses from the highlands, and, as Rikki had only arrived at Lakjamot the previous day, he had not had an opportunity to see his uncle until now.

Siggi, glad to see Rikki, bid him welcome and asked what brought him north for this visit.

Rikki answered, "I came to visit with my fylgja at Heather Hill."

Siggi said, "At least five years must have passed since you saw him the first time."

Rikki responded, "Yes, time flies by."

Siggi, smiling, asked, "Was he home?"

Rikki said, "Yes, he told me about some basic things, like how the universe is created and how we create our reality."

Siggi, ignoring the depth of the subject matter for now, asked jokingly, "How is the weather in the spiritual dimension? Was it raining?"

Rikki, smiling, responded in the same light tone, "No. It was sunny!"

After the horses were secured and the cows looked after, Siggi and Rikki, along with the rest of the family, sat around and reminisced about old times and events that had taken place since Rikki had stopped spending his summers there.

Chapter 4

Core Beliefs and Their Effect on Your Reality

THE FOLLOWING MORNING, RIKKI assisted with the morning milking before heading off again on his horse to Heather Hill. When he arrived, he made his way onto the rock and, as before, walked in circles—thrice clockwise and thrice anti-clockwise—before standing still and facing Heather Hill while thinking a loving thought of his horse, Trust. Time stood still. Heather Hill opened and Old Soul came to the door and led him into his study, and they made themselves comfortable.

Old Soul, with a smile, said, "Good morning, earthling, and welcome again to the spiritual dimension."

Rikki replied politely, "Thank you."

Old Soul continued, "Now that you understand some of the processes that take place as you create your reality, let me tell you a little bit about how you can adapt optimally to the experience of living on Earth. As I said yesterday, your thoughts go into creating your reality. It is therefore important that you have a good grasp of how your thoughts actually shape what you experience and, consequently, what you wish for. The thoughts I am referring to are underneath or behind what you normally think about, and I'll refer to them as core beliefs.

"Let me now explain in some detail how these core beliefs shape the way you perceive your world and, indeed, how they also factor in, as you create your reality."

The 'core beliefs' you have shape the way you perceive your world and have a direct influence on how you create your reality.

Rikki asked, "Is the big picture about to get even bigger?"

Old Soul said, "Life is a complicated affair, and, because it's so complicated, it is fascinating, don't you think?"

Rikki agreed. "Yes, but I'm really beginning to look forward to hearing some of your comments on the questions I had prepared for this meeting."

Old Soul said, "I know. You will actually receive the answers to most of your questions, now, as I tell you about core beliefs."

Rikki said, "Okay."

Old Soul's study was lined with bookcases, and he reached for a book on one of the shelves, placed it in his lap, and said, "Here I have a book. The title is *Core Beliefs*. Let me tell you about them."

Old Soul began, "This book explains a few fundamental features of the physical world that you must understand, accept, and work within, in order to thrive at whatever you decide to do in life."

Rikki said, "That sounds like it might be helpful in my day-to-day life."

Old Soul went on, "Yes, and as you internalize these fundamental features, a consistent set of core beliefs concerning how life unfolds on Earth will establish itself within your mind. These core beliefs will provide you with a perspective that will allow you to interpret your experiences in a way that is consistent with the basic building blocks that exist within your physical world—what I described to you yesterday."

Old Soul paused, then said, "These core beliefs will save you untold hours of unnecessary anguish, throughout the rest of your life, if you are successful at internalizing them."

Rikki, enthused, asked, "What is a core belief? Can you give me an example?"

Old Soul, smiling and with a twinkle in his eye, knowing that this would be a long lesson, replied, "I will give you numerous examples. An important aspect for you to understand is that these core beliefs that I am about to tell you about are anchored to the concept of 'meaning.'"

Rikki asked, "What do you mean by meaning?"

Old Soul continued, "Let me explain. Throughout your lifetime, events occur. You look back at these events and ask yourself *Why did this happen? What have I learned? What does this event tell me about myself as I look back on it now? In what way was it meaningful to me?* It is an automatic aspect of human nature to think about an event that has passed and to ascribe meaning to it. This, in turn, gives you a sense of purpose in the present and it helps you to feel fulfilled in the moment. This ongoing 'digestive process' of events as they pass helps you anticipate the future and move forward in life."

Rikki said, "Okay, I see."

> Life isn't about finding yourself. Life is about creating yourself.
>
> *- George Bernard Shaw*

Old Soul continued, "Now, the assignment of meaning to an event is always a subjective process. That is to say, the meaning of an event can only be discovered, or decided upon, by its owner. That is why you can never bestow meaning onto an event for another person. In other words, you can never decide for another person what is meaningful for him or her.[41]"

Rikki considered this. "Okay. I'll keep that in mind when I'm giving advice."

---

41   Victor E. Frankl. *The Will To Meaning: Foundations And Applications Of Logotherapy. New York*: Penguin Books, 1969.

Old Soul continued, "And it is through successive meaningful events that a person discovers the overall meaning of his own journey throughout his lifetime.

"Now that you understand what I mean by meaning, let me describe a few core beliefs."

Old Soul paused and said, "The concepts I'll be telling you about are fate, free will, uniqueness, action, cognitive contrast, aging, and death."

Rikki interrupted, "But we already talked about fate and free will yesterday."

Old Soul said, "Yes, but what I want to emphasize now is that you should also consider fate and free will, to be core beliefs. This will become clear as I give you some additional information about these concepts, and especially how the attitude you have toward fate and free will affect and shape the experiences you have in your daily life."

Rikki said, "Okay."

"Yesterday, I introduced these concepts from the perspective of how you construct your fate and how, by virtue of having free will, you alter your fate when you set long-term goals. I also explained how fated events are nested within the unfolding harmony and how they are carried into your present, as the unfolding harmony strings them out in the dimension of time. Now I'd like to explain these concepts from a more personalized perspective, in the hope that you can relate to them better."

Rikki said, "Okay."

Fate and the Unfolding Harmony

Old Soul continued, "There existed on Earth an unfolding synchrony and harmony of events, stretched out in the dimension of time, prior to your birth. This unfolding appears as if from the future as it comes toward you, opening windows of opportunity in the moment, before they close and disappear. If you grasp the opportunity when the window is open, then you create a history for yourself. This is the process of life that is occurring in every moment. Your birth into the physical world tossed you into this river of unfolding events.

"As you know, you are not able to see your future. Accurate predictions about what may happen aren't possible, but you can make some fairly accurate guesses about what may happen in the next few hours and less accurate guesses about events as you predict them to happen farther into the future. In a dream, you might occasionally see a brief glimpse into your future and sometimes experience it as a déjà vu experience shortly afterward, while awake.

"Clairvoyants occasionally see glimpses into the future that come true as well, but these glimpses of events, however, will never affect or change the lives of the individuals who know of them."

Rikki asked, "Why is that?"

Old Soul said, "It would undermine your *raison d'être*, your reason for living. It is crucial, in order for you to benefit fully from the experiences you

> The past is but the beginning of a beginning. And all that is and has been Is but the twilight of the dawn.
>
> *- H.G. Wells*

have set in your path, that you do not know your fate beforehand. Not knowing, allows you to experience the maximum effect of these events and to achieve the maximum amount of inner learning when they occur. You are, in fact, completely at the mercy of fate. All you can do is respond to it."

Rikki, sounding cautious, ventured, "I suppose I should brace myself for some harsh lessons in life?"

Old Soul said, "Don't forget, you also have many wonderful and joyful fated experiences ahead of you."

Rikki said, "Yes. I'm sure I do."

Old Soul continued, "Now, you have a choice. You can react in one of two ways when fate 'slaps you in the face,' so to speak. You can either choose to become better, or you can choose to become bitter. If you chose to become bitter and to engage in perpetual anguish following the fated event, then you will continue to experience the same fate again and again in a variety of different circumstances, until you learn the lesson you have intended for yourself. On the other hand, you can choose to become 'better' and to embrace the 'fated event' with a positive regard and not to anguish or worry. If you choose that course of action, than you should focus on the intended learning you set for yourself and attempt to incorporate the knowledge that fated event was meant to bring you."

Embrace fate:
Become better,
not bitter.

Rikki said, "That sounds like good advice."

Old Soul said, "Yes. And as an aid in this endeavor, it may be helpful for you to consider the idea that you can 'graduate' from a particular fate. When you graduate, that particular type of fated event ceases to derail you. The event may continue to occur, but you will stop responding to it as an obstacle in your path. You will be able to allow it to flow past, like water off a duck's back. *My advice to you is that you embrace fate and 'lovingly invite' it, knowing that it is intended as a challenge that you have given yourself. That should be a core belief.*"

Rikki echoed, "Embrace fate. That is a different way of looking at it. Most people think of fate in a negative context, as something unfortunate."

Old Soul said, "Yes, and one of the negative side effects of not embracing fate is that you will feel angry at the world and vengeful toward those individuals who were the harbingers of the fated circumstances that you yourself set in your path in the first place. But I'll tell you a little more about revenge later.

"The unfolding harmony not only coordinates the cyclic appearance of all physical events on Earth, it also coordinates the scheduling of one-time occurrences of fated events. A typical example of a fated event that was scheduled prior to your birth occurred for you in the winter after we first met. You had missed the bus that normally took you to school at 7:30 in the morning. While you waited for the next bus to arrive, an old friend of your father's, whom you had not seen for a long time, showed up. As you waited together, you conversed and told him that you would not return to your uncle's farm in the north the following summer. He told you that a friend of his, who has a farm in the south of Iceland, was looking for a farmhand. Later, after your parents had spoken, it was agreed that you would go to this farm the following summer. You have now spent five summers at this farm and have plans to continue working there for the next few summers. This was a fated occurrence set in the timeline of the unfolding harmony prior to your birth, designed to ensure that you would not spend a lifetime as a farmer at your uncle's farm."

Rikki said, "Okay, I see. But I think I would have enjoyed being a farmer."

Old Soul said, "Yes, you would have. But on a spiritual level, you know that there are other events destined for your future that will be more fulfilling. Another aspect to consider is that the unfolding harmony not only brought this fate to you, it also fulfilled your mother's wish that you not return to your uncle's farm, as well as the wish of the farmer who was looking for a farmhand in the south. This is an example of how fate comes about in life and how the unfolding harmony synchronizes and coordinates all events. One way of looking at the occurrence of fate would be to say that fate piggybacks on the unfolding harmony."

Rikki asked, "Can you help me understand a little better—what is the defining difference between 'fate' and 'unfolding harmony'?"

Old Soul said, "I know, this can be confusing. These events are intertwined, in that fated events occur within the much more expansive unfolding harmony of events. The main difference is that a fated event is initiated by your over-soul and your soul, and it is a one-time event that you scheduled to appear in the space/time line, whereas the unfolding harmony of events refers to ongoing cyclic processes, the circular patterns of the emergence and disappearance of physical structures within the world; these are directed through action by All That Is."

Rikki nodded. "Okay, I understand."

Old Soul said, "You probably realize now that nothing that happens on Earth is random. Everything is acting, in some way, on something else. Therefore, there is no such thing as pure coincidence, or luck."

There is no coincidence or luck.

Rikki asked, "What about winning at bingo or winning the lottery? Or betting on the races or on sports? Meeting your true love? People often talk about how lucky they have been, and also how unlucky they can be."

Old Soul said, "All such occurrences are fated. While most people accept that fate exists in some circumstances, like meeting their true love, whom they marry and live with 'happily ever after,' they also believe that they can be lucky, as you say, for example, at bingo or at the lottery, or at betting on the races and at sports. Luck feels more exciting and tangible than fate, and there is always a feeling that you can do something to hedge your bets. Of course, when you concentrate in order to hedge your bets, you exercise intent—which has an effect on the background canvas we spoke of earlier, which increases the likelihood that your wish will come true and that it will be brought forward via the unfolding harmony. This is the same way in which a long-term goal will materialize, as I described earlier.

"In the end, the outcome is the same. It doesn't matter whether you call it luck or fate. It's just a matter of interpretation. The result is the same. The main difference has to do with belief. A belief in fate provides for a sense of purpose and a deeper meaning in life, whereas luck suggests that whatever happens is random and that there is no greater meaning to an event."

Rikki said, "Okay, I can see that."

Old Soul continued, "You also mentioned 'bad' luck. In a similar way, in the absence of a belief in fate, bad luck is much more difficult to accept, since there is no potential meaning that can be drawn from, for example, losing all your money in a bet. Taken to the extreme, there are also broader ramifications to a belief that everything is luck, as it implies that everything that occurs is random. Your existence is a random occurrence, and there is no deeper meaning to life. People who live by this persuasion find it very difficult to recover from difficult times, if, for instance, tragedy has struck and left them bereft and feeling depressed. It is impossible for them to see meaning in life when everything that happens is random and either a consequence of good luck or of bad luck. This is why having a belief that there is fate is important. *You will thrive better if you have faith that there is fate; that should be one of your core beliefs.*"

Rikki acknowledged, "Yes, I can see how that would be helpful."

Old Soul continued, "Now let me tell you a little more about free will. I also mentioned this concept yesterday, with regard to setting long-term goals, but I want to tell you more about how you experience free will in your daily life."

Free Will

Old Soul continued his lecture. "Free will provides you with the freedom, within the confines of your fated circumstances, to do whatever you like with your life. In most cases, you intuitively know what choices to make to maximize the opportunities to learn about your inner nature and to evolve spiritually. And usually you will make the choice that leads to that positive outcome. But occasionally, you will face a dilemma, and you will not know what to do. When you are faced with such a dilemma, my advice for you is to follow your conscience and make the choice that is in accordance with the highest ideal of who you know yourself to be."

Rikki said, "Okay, I'll remember that. But what about a situation where I'm egged on by friends to do something I know is wrong?"

Old Soul said, "That can be a difficult situation. Of course, you always have free will to make the choice that is in accordance with your highest ideal. However, I know that this is not the answer you are looking for. The answer to your question has to do with strength of character, and you will learn about that when we will talk about other core beliefs later on today. For now, all I can tell you is that going against what you know is the correct thing to do will only serve to remind you of who you are *not*. It is not spiritually enlightening, since you learn nothing new about yourself. It is a backward step, and it will not advance your growth spiritually. Remember, the reason for a lifetime is to evolve spiritually. The more you go against your conscience and be 'who you are not,' the slower your spiritual ascent."

Rikki said, "Okay, I understand. But what if a person who is about to commit a crime rationalized that the act was justifiable, according to his or her conscience?"

Old Soul said, "People always have a rationale for what they do. It may be twisted, and you may not agree with it, but it's always logical to them. There is no simple answer to your question, other than to say that there are always consequences for the choices you make. And sometimes those choices will lead you to painful experiences, both for yourself and for others. These are fated events that you have placed in your path, and you know that when situations like this unfold, you will have to rise to the occasion.

"Having free will is a double-edged sword. Sometimes it's difficult to know which way to wield it. The most difficult times will occur when you are faced with what has been termed the 'divine dichotomy.'[42]"

Rikki asked, "What is that?"

Free will is a double-edged sword.

Old Soul replied, "It is when you are faced with a situation where you know that the choice you must make is against your ethics or your better judgment, yet it is the only option you have that will bring about the outcome you wish. When faced with a decision of this sort, you can be certain that you are about to learn something new about your inner nature."

Rikki commented, "That sounds heavy."

Old Soul said, "Yes it is. Intuitively, you know that, in order to evolve spiritually, you will at times have to experience both sides of the coin—how it feels to be bad and how it feels to be good; how it feels to do what you know is right and how it feels to do what you know is wrong. Or, in other words, you will sometimes have to 'be who you are not' in order to discover, on a deeper level, who you are."

---

[42] Neale Donald Welsh. *Conversations With God. Vol.1*. New York: Putnam's Sons, 1996.

Rikki said, "Isn't that the same situation I mentioned above, where you know it is a crime, but you justify it with your conscience?"

Old Soul said, "No. In this instance, the act is not premeditated. It might even be legally sanctioned, and you are compelled to act against your moral conscience. An example of the divine dichotomy in your case, for instance, would be to kill someone in self-defense, as I know you are a pacifist, or to violently attack someone who injured someone you love dearly. A general example of this often occurs during times of war, when an individual is conscripted and faced with the situation of having to kill someone for the sake of serving his country or for the greater good. When you face such a situation, you feel forced, or you are forced, to 'be who you are not.' The consequence of your act will shake you to the very core, and you may become undone. But in time, and out of the ashes, you will grow anew, with a deeper and a more profound spiritual insight, as you discover who you truly are."

Rikki said, "These lessons in life sound very difficult."

Old Soul said, "The consequences of your choices in circumstances such as these will always alter who you understand yourself to be, at your deepest level. These experiences cause you to reinvent yourself, having attained an 'inner experience' that would otherwise not have been possible. Similar experiences of self-discovery, or inner learning, occur more commonly following personal relationship disasters, where, in hindsight you discover that you had to cause a lot of pain, both to yourself and to others, in order to figure out who you were. These experiences cause your world to shift, and you realize afterward that the things that mattered before are completely different from what matters after the experience; you view your life through a different lens. You feel different, and you know that your values have changed in some fundamental way."

Rikki queried, "What types of personal relationship disasters are you referring to?"

Old Soul said, "There are many—those that occur through physical abuse, sexual abuse, alcohol abuse, drug abuse, betrayal in relationships. Situations in which your free will leads to disastrous consequences. These experiences are fated, and it is the individual's responsibility in his journey of self-discovery to discover 'who he is not,' by exercising his free will and making choices that lead him to be a better human being, in accordance with his highest ideals."

Rikki sighed. "Life can be hard."

Old Soul said, "Yes . . . and blissfully beautiful as well. Fortunately, most people do not encounter the worst of these situations during their lifetimes."

Old Soul continued, "Now that we have looked at fate and free will in some detail, let's turn our attention to the concept of uniqueness. I mentioned this concept to you yesterday, in terms of how it plays a role in creating your reality. But let's look at it from a more personal perspective today."

Rikki agreed, "Okay."

Uniqueness

Old Soul continued to speak. "You are unique. That is one of the most important concepts I'll be explaining to you today. You, of course, know intuitively that you are unique, but you must bring it into your conscious awareness in your daily life. Remind yourself of this fact often throughout the day. It also follows that, because you're unique, you are also irreplaceable. No one can replace the unique contribution you bring into the physical world. All human beings are unique, none are identical. In fact, there have never been two identical human beings, ever, in the history of man—and there never will be in the future. *It is fundamental for you to remember at all times that you are unique and therefore irreplaceable.*[43] *This must be a core belief in order for you to thrive."*

You're unique and irreplaceable

Rikki agreed. "Okay, I'm unique and irreplaceable. I'll make that my mantra."

Old Soul said, "Good idea. The next concept has to do with action. I've mentioned 'action' before in regards to movement within the universe. But there is a more personal aspect to action as well, once again, in terms of your daily life."

Action

Old Soul continued, "You already know that you made the decision to have a lifetime on Earth in order to learn about your inner nature. You also know that this learning takes place when you create emotions within yourself, as a consequence of your interactions with others. You now also know that you are unique. Given these conditions, it follows that your most fundamental responsibility to yourself (and to others, as they learn from their interactions with you) is to act, or to take action, during your incarnation. Think of yourself as a flower that blossoms. Open your petals, and embrace your life. You have a finite lifetime to absorb all that you can.

> Put not off from day to day and from cycle to cycle, in the belief that ye will succeed in obtaining the mysteries when ye return to the world in another cycle.
>
> *- Jesus Christ (From the Gnostic scripture, Pistis Sophia)*

So, take action and be yourself unapologetically. *You can only learn about your inner nature through your actions. This must be a core belief."*

---

[43]   Victor E. Frankl. *The Will To Meaning: Foundations And Applications Of Logotherapy.* New York: Penguin Books, 1969.

Rikki responded, "Okay. I'm unique and irreplaceable, and I'll take action and be myself unapologetically."

Old Soul said, "Good."

Rikki then asked, "What if people don't like me and they judge me?"

Act. Be yourself unapologetically.

Old Soul said, "There will always be people who will like you and others who will not. Remember, you are unique. It is also normal for people to form opinions and to make judgments about each other. I'll be telling you much more about these topics later on, so be patient. For now, my only advice to you is: Don't judge yourself, leave it to others; consider that what other people think of you is none of your business."

Rikki, smiling hesitantly, said, "Okay, I'll work on that."

Old Soul said, "Now, the next concept is an interesting one. This I refer to as 'cognitive contrast.'"

Cognitive Contrast

Old Soul continued, "You will remember that I told you a little bit about physical contrast yesterday, in terms of how the body is able to perceive physical experiences. Another important feature of contrast relates to the uniqueness of your thoughts. You know, because you are unique, that no one on Earth has had exactly the same experiences in life as you have had, and therefore, no one has the same perspective. It is therefore a given that your thoughts, attitudes, ideas, and personal beliefs about everything are unique in some way, and they are therefore in contrast with those of others.

"As I've said before, you are on Earth to learn, and you have an implicit agreement with all other humans you encounter to give of yourself to them, just as they give of themselves to you. Therefore, your most basic responsibility while on Earth is to thrust your uniqueness into this world. Your contribution will help others, as your thoughts are in contrast to theirs. It is through this contrast that they are able to assess their own thoughts and understand their own uniqueness. In other words, by speaking up and communicating your thoughts, you provide a yardstick for others that they can use to formulate their own thoughts, in terms of how they contrast with yours. Do you follow, so far?"

Rikki replied, "Yes, I understand."

Old Soul continued, "You should also understand that on the most fundamental level, all humans are equally valid and all thoughts and ideas are equally valid.[44] It would be incorrect of you to think, in the context in which we are speaking, that your thoughts or ideas are superior to someone else's or that one human being makes a more valid contribution to the world than another."

> All humans are equally valid, and all thoughts and ideas are equally valid.

Rikki said, "I understand."

Old Soul said, "Also, while speaking your mind, don't hesitate because you think you are wrong about something. There is no thought or idea that is 'right' or 'wrong', per se.[45] The objective

---

[44] Victor E. Frankl. *The Will To Meaning: Foundations And Applications Of Logotherapy.* NewYork: Penguin Books, 1969.

[45] Neale Donald Welsh. *Conversations With God. Vol.1.* New York: Putnam's Sons, 1996.

is to arrive at a solution that best fits a specific situation, and, consequently, leads to maximum harmony. So, for example, in a circumstance where a decision needs to be made about an issue, it is the contribution of each different thought or idea that provides the contrast, thus paving the way for a process of evaluation between contrasting thoughts and ideas to take place and for a consensus to develop on an issue that best fits a given circumstance. It is not important that your contribution be the 'right' one or the one that is consistent with the final consensus. A 'wrong' thought in this instance, or a thought that does not fit, is equally valid, since without it, a discussion as to how it does not fit could not take place. And by the same token, the appreciation of the accuracy of the 'best fitting' thought, or idea, would not have been possible."

Rikki commented, "Speaking up is not easy for everyone, especially when their self-worth is at zero. My friend prefers to fade into the background, rather than to speak up and be noticed. Afterward, he castigates himself for a missed opportunity to speak his mind or to make a comment."

Old Soul replied, "You are right. For many, it is very difficult to speak up, to be themselves unapologetically, and to act into the world, which is indeed their most basic responsibility to account for their lives. Some have difficulty believing that their contribution is worthy. I have a suggestion for your friend the next time he finds himself in a situation like this."

Rikki asked, "Okay. What's that?"

Old Soul said, "Ask him to concentrate on the fact that every utterance he makes to another person is a gift from him to them. A unique gift that can only be given by him, as indeed, he is unique. To help him along with this task, ask him to think of his favorite food. What is his favorite dish? He might say, 'I like my mother's spaghetti. It is the best ever!' Then tell him, the next time he is hesitant to speak up, to visualize that he is giving his audience, or the person he is talking to, his mother's spaghetti. It is the best spaghetti ever, it is his unique gift to them, and it is irreplaceable.

This will aid him as he practices overcoming his hesitancy and to speak up, unapologetically."

Rikki said with a smile, "That sounds funny, but it's a good idea. I'll tell him."

Old Soul went on, "Finally, you must understand that this talk about contrasting thoughts must not be confused with competition or with power. Your objective, in the context we have discussed, should not be driven by a motivation to be better than someone else or to stand out. And it should not be to achieve power and control. We are only talking about unique contributions. *In order to thrive, you must embrace your uniqueness and the contrast your thoughts and ideas provide for others. It is important that this is established as a core belief."*

Rikki said, "Okay, I understand. You are not trying to educate me about competition or power."

Old Soul said, "That's correct."

Rikki was gradually becoming more and more intrigued, as a framework about how the physical world was put together, how it operated, how he created his experience within it, and how these specific tools prescribed by core beliefs, seemed to provide some practical concepts he could actually put to use in his daily life.

Old Soul continued, "There is more. Now let me tell you about aging. Growing older is another aspect of physical life that people often have difficulty accepting."

Aging

Old Soul kept speaking. "It's important for everyone to accept that life on Earth is finite. As with all circular process originating in the conscious canvas, and emerging into your physical world through the unfolding harmony, your body grows from seed, ages, and withers, until it is no longer sustainable, and it dies. This aging process is difficult for many to accept, and people will go to extreme lengths to alter their bodies so as to appear younger. While youthful looks are cherished in Western culture, it is ultimately important to accept that *the aging process is normal and inevitable. This needs to be a core belief."*

Life on Earth is finite: You grow from seed, age, wither, and die.

Rikki interjected, "This does not worry me—yet!"

Old Soul said, smiling, "At the age of seventeen, it shouldn't, but you are likely to wish for youth as you become older.

"We are almost finished for today. I'll conclude by making a few comments about death."

Rikki said, "Okay."

Death

"Remember that because of the symbiotic relationship your body has with your soul, your body will die when you withdraw from it. Most people do not know the exact time of their death, but their over-soul and their soul, usually unbeknownst to the outer ego, and sometimes unbeknownst to the inner identity as well, make the decision sometime beforehand. *There are therefore no accidental deaths, as far as the over-soul and the soul are concerned.* Souls choose the circumstances of their exit for their own experience—and also in agreement with loved ones, who have chosen to experience their subsequent grief, for their own development," Old Soul explained.

Rikki commented, "I would like to know sometime before I die, when that will happen."

Old Soul said, "Maybe you will know that. I am not permitted to tell you that information. Most deaths occur at the end of the body's natural lifecycle. In these instances, the soul may select to experience an illness as a means of death, if the experience of having an illness is wanted. At other times, the body will simply collapse and die, usually during sleep. Some souls choose to exit earlier on in life, for various reasons, but this is always followed by a decision on a spiritual level that is based on a joint decision between the soul that wishes to leave and the over-souls and souls of their contemporaries who will mourn them."

Rikki said, "I don't think that people experiencing grief would normally agree with that."

Old Soul continued, "No, it's a concept that is difficult for most people to hear and to accept. Having this knowledge and knowing that your soul will not die, however, will not prevent you from experiencing the full force of grief when someone close to you dies. It is natural for all humans to grieve the loss of someone they love. But it should, however, give you some peace to know that your loved one has merely crossed over into this spiritual dimension, perfectly intact cognitively and emotionally, and with all their memories. And you, too, will inevitably follow. *Understanding this spiritual process of how and when death occurs should be a core belief, in order for you to work effectively through your unavoidable feelings of grief.*

There are no accidental deaths.

"It is always sad for survivors to cope with the inevitable loss when people die, whether it be in old age, early in life, or unexpectedly. But keep in mind, your world is an arena where souls design the circumstances that will give them the experiences that will allow them to create their own emotions in response to those experiences. This is the main reason for having a physical life in the first place. It is in this way that souls learn about themselves as they experience successive lifetimes. They do this, for example, by taking turns at being a victor or a villain, a helper or a hinderer, a student or a teacher, a patient or a doctor, a father or a son—and to experience the emotional roller coaster that these roles give rise to. The accumulation of these multiple roles through lifetimes allows the over-soul to learn and experience firsthand the many facets of all emotional states. It is through this experience that over-souls evolve, as they slowly drift toward an ever increasing harmony with All That Is."

Rikki said, "So was someone like Hitler a good man or a bad man? Was he a villain, simply for the experience?"

Old Soul said, "You have picked a controversial topic. And it is a topic of special interest to you, although you are not aware of that on a conscious level."

Rikki asked, "What do you mean?"

Old Soul said, "Well, your most recent lifetime was as a Polish Jew. Your wife and two children were killed in the bombing raids on Krakow in 1939, and you were shot in the back of the head shortly afterward by the Gestapo."

Rikki, eyes wide open, asked incredulously, "What? Is that true?"

Old Soul said quietly, "Yes it is. That is one reason for your pacifism. You've recently experienced war firsthand, and you have no appetite for reliving the inhumanity that is perpetrated in those situations."

Rikki said, "Oh, my goodness."

Old Soul continued, "Yes. I will tell you a little more about how that life has affected your current incarnation, later on."

Rikki breathed, "I look forward to that."

Old Soul said, "Now, in answer to your question about Hitler. Remember, you live in two worlds simultaneously, so there are two answers to your question: one from the perspective of your life on Earth and the other from the perspective of your life in the spiritual dimension. As you currently reside on Earth, you should focus on what would be the most adaptive course of action within the physical world. The boundaries of what is considered acceptable behavior are reflections of the values, the ethics, and the morals of your culture. And you have laws that are derived from these precepts. In the case of Hitler, his actions caused emotional pain, not only for thousands of individuals, but for the entire Western civilization. And you have no choice but to judge him and other similarly barbaric individuals within the context of your cultural values and ethics. Passing judgment isn't easy, however, because it is also true that Hitler and the culture that supported him at that time believed that they were acting in accordance with their highest ideals, and that their actions were justified. That is a truth in all instances of this sort. Dictators always justify their actions by a rationale that is a reflection of their highest ideals. Inevitably, however, you cannot escape from forming an opinion and making a judgment based on your own values, ethics, and morals, within the context of your culture."

Rikki said, "It is difficult for me to accept that a whole nation's highest ideals would be to exterminate Jews, homosexuals, disabled people, and those who are mentally challenged."

Old Soul said, "Not everyone in Germany voted for the Nazi Party, and many who did never anticipated that the party's ideals would lead to such atrocities."

Rikki asked, "How can souls and over-souls, while knowing the future, be responsible for such carnage?"

Old Soul said, "Wars have ravaged the Earth for centuries. The emotional experience of horror and loss are part of the journey that souls elect to experience in order to evolve."

Old Soul continued, "Let me return to the topic of death. As I said earlier, no death is an accident. However, sudden death may still come as a shock and be resisted by the outer ego and by the inner identity of someone who is not prepared to die or who is afraid to die. In those cases, the entire consciousness may not ascend into the spiritual dimension at the time of death."

Rikki said, "I remember my Uncle Siggi mentioning something about that a few years ago, when we were walking one of the cows over to a nearby farm to get impregnated."

Old Soul said, "You are correct. Your uncle described some of these types of occurrences when you were twelve, but I'll review them for you again and add a little more information to what he told you."

Spirit Entities

"The journey over into the spiritual dimension is normally easy. At the time of death, a final copy of all experiences and memories the person has are reviewed in rapid succession[46], as the soul prepares to reunite with the over-soul. At that time, the outer ego and the inner identity are absorbed by the soul. In rare instances, however, things do not go as planned, and portions of the inner identity and the outer ego are not absorbed by the soul. They splinter off and hover in a state of limbo within the Earth plane, outside the dimension of time. These fragments retain memories and experiences of the person they were as human beings, and they are usually referred to as entities, spirit entities, or ghosts," Old Soul explained.

"When this occurs, one of at least three scenarios may have taken place:

[46] Van Pim Lommel. *Consciousness Beyond Life*. New York: Harper Collins, 2010.

- The person who died might have had a strong attachment to some unfinished business on Earth that he or she feels compelled to attend to before allowing himself or herself to ascend into the spiritual dimension.[47] These individuals are usually referred to as ghosts. They are not aware of the passage of time and may continue to linger for untold years, often in a state of frustration, until they find peace, at which time they ascend into the spiritual dimension and reunite with their over-soul.

- The person might have committed a dreadful deed and he or she is afraid to ascend into the spiritual dimension for fear of retribution. These entities may be malevolent. Some of them enjoy taking advantage of unsuspecting people for their own gain, manipulating them and attempting to control them.

- In yet another instance, the person may simply be in shock, unaware—or not accepting—that the body has perished. These entities wander around as if in a fog, unawares, until they are made aware of what has happened to them. As they wander about, they find themselves attracted to the aura of individuals who share similar emotions as they had just prior to death. When they encounter a suitable host, they attach themselves, or take up lodging, in that person's aura and stay there until they are woken up and made aware of what has happened to their own physical bodies."

Rikki asked, "How does that happen? Who wakes them up and makes them aware?"

---

[47] Interesting books on this subject, include: Carl Wickland. *Thirty Years Among The Dead*. Pomeroy: National Psychological Institute. First print in 1924; reprinted 1963. Also, William J. Baldwin. *Spirit Releasement Therapy: A Technique Manual*. Terra Alta: Headline Books, 1992.

Old Soul said, "Occasionally the host will go to a therapist who has training in these matters and is able to 'release' the entity and direct it into the spiritual dimension. Usually, however, the entity remains with the host until that person dies and crosses over, at which time he or she follows the host into the spiritual dimension. On other occasions, the entity is assisted into the spiritual dimension by a 'rescue soul.' Some souls here in the spiritual dimension specifically engage themselves as rescue souls."

Rikki asked, "What happens when an entity latches itself onto someone's aura?"

Old Soul answered, "This is a good question. The entity which is as if in a sleep is usually unaware, but the host usually experiences a sudden change in health or behavior. This happens because the emotions that were heightened at the time of the entity's death, be it from addiction, illness, or an accident, are transferred to the host. So, for example, if the entity was an alcoholic or a cigarette smoker, the host might suddenly begin to crave large amounts of alcohol or suddenly develop a craving for cigarettes. Similarly, if the person died from a heart attack or an illness that caused him to experience pain, than the host may suddenly begin to experience these painful symptoms in the corresponding parts of his or her body. And finally, if the entity died in an accident, for example in traffic, in a fire, or by drowning, then the host may suddenly begin to fear these situations. The good news is that when these entities are released, the associated symptoms disappear instantly."

Rikki asked, "Do these entities have a soul?"

Old Soul said, "The soul is never damaged, and it cannot be fragmented in any way. It always ascends, complete, when the body dies. However, as I said earlier, the inner identity and the outer ego may not be completely absorbed into the soul before it ascends. These aspects, or fragments of the person, retain the person's memories as well as the person's identity. Their conscious awareness, or soul quality, ranges from being very limited to appearing to be almost fully intact. A ghost, for example, will generally have a very limited conscious awareness. That is why they are usually seen to be engaged in repetitive acts that are focused on a specific intent, presumably to resolve some unfinished business. The malevolent entity, on the other hand, appears more intelligent and has a more expansive consciousness, but it is also limited."[48]

Rikki murmured, "Okay, I see."

"Finally, I'll tell you about one additional, somewhat unrelated, circumstance that is not uncommon, but that occurs sometimes following an abortion or a miscarriage. Of course, in all of these instances, the soul is fully aware beforehand that the fetus will not be carried to term."

Rikki, interrupting, asked; "Do souls know beforehand that they will be aborted? Some people consider an abortion as no different from premeditated murder."

Old Soul said, "I know that this is a controversial topic, but we are talking from the perspective of the soul in this context, and, as you know, the soul exists outside the dimension of time, and it knows exactly what will happen next. For people on Earth, however, as I said earlier—you cannot help being a product of your culture and of the prevailing attitudes and beliefs that exist within it. You have no choice but to form opinions based on your point of view. The ultimate truth is not so important here; remember, it is the emotions that you create that are what life is all about. It is through them that you learn about your inner nature."

Rikki asked again, "So there is not right or wrong opinion here?"

Old Soul said patiently, "No, it is only what works for you in terms of creating the emotional experiences that you need to learn about your inner nature."

---

[48] For a good documentation of this type of entity, please see: Joe Fisher. *The Siren Call Of Hungry Ghosts*. New York: Para View Press, 2001.

Old Soul continued, "But let me get back on topic. A soul that has not been incarnated on a physical planet before will often choose to have the experience of a temporary gestation, in order to have the experience and to practice melding with the consciousness of the fetus and forming the inner identity and the outer ego prior to birth. This experience provides valuable practice if the soul intents to become incarnate on Earth in the future. Following the termination of the pregnancy, the soul might also choose to continue working with a simulated version of a physical body, in which case an aura that simulates the physical body continues to develop and mature here in the spiritual dimension. Your 'spirit' brother, whom your mother had to abort late in her pregnancy and who often visits you as you are about to fall asleep, is a good example of this type of soul. He is growing up in the spiritual dimension, with an aura similar to that of a human being and on a simulated timeline."

Rikki said, "Thank you. That was one of my questions."

Old Soul said, "Yes, I know."

Old Soul now leaned back into his easy chair and said, "Now you have it. I have reviewed some basic aspects, or concepts, of reality. Yesterday we reviewed concepts that relate more to physical aspects, and today we looked at concepts that are mainly anchored in meaning. All of what I've told you is factual and occurs within the physical world. I am certain that you will find it beneficial if you allow this information to comprise the platform of core beliefs upon which you build your experience."

Rikki responded solemnly, "Okay, I'll try to do that."

Old Soul continued, "You may be interested to know that most people's psychological problems stem from the fact that, in their formative years, they were not made aware of these basic principles. So, as they grew up, some of them formed false core beliefs, based on misconceptions and misunderstandings about how to operate in the world. And, as their experiences accumulated and were consistently misinterpreted over time, deep-seated emotional conflicts began to occur and to fester. The sad truth is that these conflicts would not have occurred had they been instructed to internalize these core beliefs that I have told you about, at the outset."

Rikki said, "I see."

Old Soul continued, "Once false core beliefs are established, skewed interpretations of physical existence begin to build up over time, and as this happens, psychological conflicts begin to occur. Unfortunately, it is very difficult for a person to undo years of misattributions made on the basis of false core beliefs. Therapeutic assistance is therefore often required."

Rikki wondered aloud, "I wonder how many false core beliefs I have?"

Old Soul said, "You will do well if you think about what I have said and make an attempt to internalize these concepts. These aspects about how the world is made up, your place in it, and how you interpret your existence, need to become your second nature, a lens through which you interpret and understand your reality."

Rikki said, "Okay, I'll work on it and talk to my friends about it."

Old Soul said, "That will be good."

Old Soul continued, "We have covered a lot of information, yet I know that you have some general questions about life and death, as well as questions about personal issues regarding your sexual orientation, for which you'd like my advice."

Rikki said gratefully, "Yes, your advice would be much appreciated."

Old Soul said, "I am aware of your questions and your concerns. As you think about what we have discussed today and yesterday, you will realize, however, that you already have answers to your questions regarding the unexpected deaths of young individuals.

You now also know that the illness that caused the paralysis and mental delay for the two boys at the farm was a choice their souls made in order to gain that unique perspective in life. Individuals who are either mentally or physically disabled from birth usually do not suffer during their lifetimes, provided they receive adequate care. The anguish and sadness over their condition is more often created within the hearts of those who love and care for them, and it is through their compassion that the opportunity is created for them to discover something about their own inner natures."

Rikki said, "It just seems so unfair for those little boys. I have a lot of difficulty helping out with their care when I'm at the farm. I somehow can't relate to them, and so I don't like it when I'm asked to look after them."

Old Soul said, "Well, don't worry yourself about that. The reason has to do with a past life you had that you haven't worked through adequately."

Rikki asked, "Another past life? What was this one?"

Old Soul said, "It was a short life in Europe in the seventeen hundreds. You were a mentally delayed boy. You had been abandoned by your parents, who were very poor. You scrounged for a living and died at the age of nine, when a horse drawn wagon knocked you down. Your body was thrown out with the garbage."

Rikki said, "Oh. I suppose I somehow see a reflection of myself in their experience."

Old Soul said, "Yes. Fortunately, these boys receive much better care than you did."

Old Soul continued, "The car accident that left your friend paralyzed was also a fate that he elected to experience, in order to learn from the challenges that that type of injury presented to him. And the individuals who loved him, including you, also elected to have that emotional experience, in order to learn something about your own inner natures."

Rikki said, "Yes, I understand. But it's upsetting for me to think about him."

Rikki was beginning to wonder whether Old Soul was going to give him some direction with regard to his own sexual orientation.

Old Soul continued, "My advice to you with regard to your sexual orientation must, however, wait. Trust me, your life is unfolding in exactly the way you planned it, prior to your birth. There are some difficult times for you ahead, and I will guide you through them the best I can, but only enough so as not to undo the impact that the experiences you have elected are meant to have,"

Rikki replied, somewhat disappointed, "Okay, I understand. Will I be okay?"

Old Soul said, "Yes, but that is all I can tell you at this time. Our visit must now come to an end, but I will continue to support you from afar. We will meet again in the not-too-distant future, at which time I will give you important information with regard to your sexual orientation, as well as on a number of other issues. Thank you for your visit. My thoughts are always with you."

Rikki stood up and thanked Old Soul. Old Soul showed him to the portal, which swept Rikki back out into the physical world. And, as before, no clock time had passed, whereas in terms of Rikki's personal experience of the passage of time, it felt as if several hours had gone by.

After collecting his thoughts for a few minutes, Rikki mounted his horse and rode toward the farm. He felt older and more wise. His perspective on life and how he would apply himself had shifted after his first visit with Old Soul, five years earlier, and now, once again, after these two visits, he felt that he had a new lease on life.

As Rikki rode back to the farm, he began to ponder what his relationship actually was with Old Soul. Old Soul certainly appeared to be a true friend. Maybe they had known each other as souls, prior to his birth? As he continued to juggle this thought in his mind, he arrived at the perimeter of the turf/stone wall that formed a fence around the west side of the lawn that surrounded the farm.

He was distracted by a truck from the local abattoir that had pulled up to the corral up ahead, in preparation for loading some young foals.

———◆———

Rikki returned home and started school a few days later, more determined than ever. The first few days of class were stressful. That year, he began to attend a different school in downtown Reykjavik with a new group of students. It was a four-year course that focused on preparing students for university. This new school was housed in an old building located next to the lake, in the center of old Reykjavik. There were twenty students to a class, seated in four rows, two to a table. The teacher's desk was at the front of the classroom, with a large blackboard on the wall behind. There were windows on the left side, with a view out over the lake, and a hallway outside the entrance along the right wall. Rikki was seated beside a six-foot-tall boy named Alfred. He had good looks, dark brown hair, and unusually nice eyes. Alfred was a frustratingly studious guy, in Rikki's opinion. But because of that, he had honed some good study habits, and his grades were always good—unlike Rikki's. They became good friends, and he frequently assisted Rikki with his studies, both in class and after school.

Rikki continued to be enthusiastic about what he had learned from Old Soul, and he attempted to put these concepts into practice during the school year, as he had promised. The fifteen-minute recess periods were a good opportunity for his explorations. During these times, Rikki often managed to mention one of the concepts he had learned from Old Soul in conversation, in order to test out his thoughts. For example, on one occasion, he said, "You know, Alfred, I feel unique and irreplaceable today."

Alfred responded, "What do you mean by that?"

Rikki answered, "Well, there is no one just like me anywhere in the world. I'm unique, and therefore, I am irreplaceable."

Alfred said, "I suppose that makes two of us!"

Rikki continued, "My presence is a gift. Every word I utter adds to your world."

Alfred rejoined, "And so do my words add to yours!"

Rikki, determined not to let it go, continued. "Every point of view I describe to you enables you to contrast it with what you might be thinking and to discover how you are different from me."

Alfred, with a smile said, "I thank God when I discover how different I am from you."

Rikki replied, also smiling, "And so do I."

In this way, and throughout the school year, Rikki practiced the concepts Old Soul had told him about. Alfred was a good sport and indulged Rikki's antics as he attempted to put Old Soul's concepts into practice.

Rikki said one day, "Today, I feel like a flower, blossoming, spreading my petals unapologetically into the world for everyone to see."

Alfred, being a rather reserved type of guy, replied, "Why would you want to do that?"

Rikki said in response, "It is my first and most basic responsibility, in order to account for my life, for my existence. It's a gift. A gift from me to you; as you are a gift to me. To be or not to be. That is the question, and the challenge."

Alfred said to him, "There you go again. It sounds like you're proposing to me!"

Rikki, smiling, said, "The truth leaks out from my every pore."

And so it went on. As the weeks went by, Rikki practiced the concepts Old Soul had told him about. This spiritual existential philosophy began to have a positive influence on the attitude he took toward his life. The hesitant attitude that had developed due to his early struggles with stammering and academic difficulties began to be replaced by an inner confidence. The more he attempted to internalize the core beliefs and understand the frame of reference they provided for his life, the better he seemed able to function. Life wasn't necessarily easy, but the essential tools given to him by these core beliefs allowed him to navigate more easily through the ups and downs that he was experiencing. He wondered why this had never been taught at school. *Surely every young pupil would benefit from an understanding of these core beliefs,* he thought.

He discovered how to overcome the habit of withdrawing in social situations and of feeling apologetic. He knew now that there was no reason for him to continue to feel that way, but it wasn't easy to break the habit, especially when faced with circumstances in which he felt uncertain. So he began to remind himself, every time he felt that way, that he was unique and irreplaceable. Being wrong about something and not coming up with the best idea was okay, because at the very least, it added a contrasting perspective to a conversation; not knowing was as valid as knowing. There were numerous challenges, though, like asking questions in class when he did not understand what the teacher was saying. And little things, like having the confidence to answer the phone at his part-time job, even though he might not know the answer to a question that might be asked of him.

Then there was fate. Old Soul had advised that he embrace fate. So, one day at school during recess, after Alfred had been lamenting about some trivial misfortune, Rikki commented, "You know, you asked for this to happen!"

Alfred's reply, anticipating another uncalled-for morsel of wisdom, was, "What? I never asked for this to happen. What do you mean?"

Rikki asked him, "Well, what do you think life is about?"

Alfred took a few seconds to think and replied, "Learning, having experiences?"

Rikki said, "Exactly. Your misfortune was a learning experience, wasn't it?"

Alfred said, "Yes, but I did not ask for it. It must have been God's will."

Rikki said, "Do you think that God wants to upset you?"

Alfred said, "Well, no. I think I'm a pretty nice guy."

Rikki responded, "So, why do you think he would do that? You have to think outside the box. Maybe you planned this yourself, in order to learn from it; to discover how you would deal with it; to learn about yourself. You just said that life is about learning and experiencing."

Alfred said slowly, "Yes?"

Rikki continued, "Look at it this way. Your soul is eternal, but your body isn't. Before your body was born, you made plans for this life. You had specific objectives about what you wanted to learn. You placed certain events in your path that you knew would come your way during your lifetime. These events are fated to occur;

they're your fate. Now you must discover what it was you meant for yourself to learn."

Alfred smiled sheepishly; "Okay, I see what you are saying. But I don't like it. Life isn't fair!"

Just then, the bell rang, ending recess. As Alfred turned to enter the classroom, he commented, "You know, none of us are going to get out of this alive!"

Rikki, smiled, "What?! Of course not!"

Chapter 5

Wake-up Call

R IKKI DIDN´T RETURN TO Holar the following spring; he began to
work on hot-water drilling rigs instead. These rigs were located
in numerous areas of Iceland where natural thermal energy can
be found, and hot water is piped into homes for heating. The rigs
normally had a crew of a half-dozen men working on twelve hours
shifts, so the drilling continued uninterrupted. The drilling rigs
were mobile and usually mounted on the backs of large, heavy
trucks. Rikki's job, as the mast man, was to guide the pipes as they
were lowered into the boreholes and subsequently heaved out, to
replace the diamond drill heads that wore out after boring through
layers of rock. When the boreholes were deep enough, they'd
reach the hot steam aquifers, from which steam, at temperatures
in the range of two hundred degrees Celsius, gushed up.

The crew worked for three weeks and then took a week off for rest.
The work was challenging and could be dangerous, but the money
was good. And for the first time in his life Rikki had loads of money
to burn, so he spent his weeks off partying with his friends. Rikki,
who had not begun to drink alcohol until the age of seventeen,
figured he had plenty of catching up to do.

Prior to that time, Rikki had spent most Saturday nights at a dance
hall for teetotalers with a couple of friends, dancing the nights away
to accordion music and folk dances. They referred to themselves
as The Three Musketeers as they joked around and pranced around
the dance floor, tiptoeing like antelopes one dance after the other,
all night long. These were good times. Toward the end of that
period, Rikki began to smuggle booze into the dance hall, stuffed
into the crotch of his pants, as that was the only area of the body
the security personnel did not frisk when guests arrived. On one
such occasion, Rikki had stuffed a mickey of homemade brew into
his pants, but he forgot about it after entering the dance hall. The
brew was a fresh batch, and the fermentation hadn't quite settled,
so the pressure in the bottle built up. And as usual, after arriving,
he began to dance with abandon, swinging around, doing polkas
and other energetic dances, and, all the while, the mead warmed

up and shook around in his crotch. Suddenly the flask burst, much to his chagrin. Fortunately, no vital organs were cut or damaged in this incident, but suffice it to say, this was one of the last times he attended the teetotaler's dance.

The parties continued with increased frequency following the summer months and into the winter, after school began. Rikki's grades began to drop, and eventually, at the age of eighteen, he failed his entire grade and was forced to repeat the school year. This was a wake-up call. It dawned on him that he'd never make it to university unless he pulled himself together and took better control of all the after-hours socializing.

It was obvious to him that his frequent late-night carousing had a lot to do with being in the closet about his sexual orientation. But he saw no alternative. Rikki felt that being openly gay in Iceland at that time was not an option.

About this time, Rikki began to feel increasingly confined within the shores of Iceland, and he worried about the lack of career opportunities he might have, especially if his sexual orientation should be discovered. He had increasingly been having sex and spending the nights with men, and he knew that it was only a matter to time before his sexual preference would become common knowledge.

Rikki's boyhood interest in becoming a veterinarian had been replaced some time ago with a decision to study medicine. Recent escapades, however, had begun to steer him away from this goal. He decided that a fresh start would be in order, and for that, the best option would be to attend university abroad, rather than in Iceland. This would also give him an opportunity to conceal his homosexuality a little longer. Having fixed his mind on

> Your work is going to fill a large part of your life, and the only way to be truly satisfied is to do what you believe is great work. And the only way to do great work is to love what you do. If you haven't found it yet, keep looking.
>
> - *Steve Jobs*

the goal of moving abroad, he knew that he needed better grades to be admitted into university. So, with determination, he buckled down and repeated the school year. He applied to university, got accepted into a two-year pre-med program, and left Iceland for Canada in the fall of 1972, at the age of twenty.

There was a condition, however. In order to be accepted into medical school following the pre-med program, Rikki's marks had to be straight A's. But things did not unfold as expected. Culture shock and poor English skills took their toll, and his grades were very poor the first semester. In fact, psychology was the only course he passed, out of a total of six courses on his roster. His plan to pursue medicine was no longer an option, and he had to decide on a new course of action.

These were difficult times. Rikki was shocked. Once again, he had failed—almost as dramatically as when he failed his entire grade a couple of years earlier. But the saving grace this time around was that none of his boyhood friends knew about it. Life was a struggle, but Rikki had grown used to struggling academically from the time he was a little boy. Of course, he wondered: *Why this fate? Had he wished for this to happen?* He recalled that Old Soul had once suggested that he'd work as a therapist, but Rikki had assumed it was in the context of being a medical doctor.

After reeling for a couple of weeks, he decided to embrace his fate and become 'better' rather than 'bitter,' as Old Soul had once advised. Rikki had to set a new long-term goal. Psychology seemed the most reasonable option, given the circumstances, so he decided to become a psychologist.

Rikki gradually found his footings, and, with his new determination, his grades began to climb. He enjoyed psychology. The long-term goal gave purpose to his work, fulfillment in the moment, and meaning in hindsight, as he applied himself single-mindedly to achieving his goal. University agreed with him. He excelled and completed one degree after another—a bachelor's degree, a master's degree, and an internship in clinical psychology.

Soon, eight years had passed since Rikki had left Iceland. These years had been busy, and he had spent many hours at the library poring over books on weekends and late into the evenings. During this time, Rikki had continued to keep his romantic thoughts to himself, and he stayed in the closet, fearing discrimination. The last hurdle was to be accepted into a PhD program. After that, he thought it would be safe to come out of the closet!

By that time, Rikki had grown weary of living in Canada and wished once again to go somewhere else. This time, his choice was England. He applied to York University and, lo and behold, he was accepted. The goal of becoming a psychologist was in sight, and all he had to do was to keep his nose to the ground and work hard to complete his degree. Now, finally, he felt safe to come out of the closet.

His new professor at York, his professor during his internship, and his professor from his master's degree studies had all known one another in the early thirties, when they studied psychology at the same university in London. But they had all lost contact and not communicated since that time. They were not aware of the connection that had occurred through Rikki's academic career until he pointed it out to them. When he realized the connection, Rikki thought to himself that this was an example of 'good' fate. He marveled at the guidance he had received and was about to receive from these three university friends from long ago. He knew now that there was no such thing as true coincidence. The only explanation could be that their presence in his life was fated. *Had he contacted them prior to birth? Were they strategically fated to appear on his path to support him on his journey through university?* He decided to ask Old Soul about that sometime.

Coming Out and Sexuality

Rikki finally dared to come out of the closet. This was a relief. Since the age of seven, he did not remember a single day that he had not had a romantic crush on someone. Some of these infatuations lasted a few months and others a year or two, but they all tore at his heartstrings and caused him endless hours of anguish. His romantic feelings always focused on a heterosexual friend where, as Rikki began to realize, his needs would never be met. Rikki's love for some of his friends was returned through intimacy in friendship, and very occasionally in sexual situations, when they were sufficiently inebriated after a late night on the town, but never romantically. In hindsight, he understood that these friendships had been safe, as no chance of real love was ever possible, and he never had to confront his sexual orientation openly. He had been safe in the closet.

Now, after jumping through the last academic hurdle, he relaxed. It was safe to fall in love, to be himself, and to be gay without fear of jeopardizing his most cherished goal of becoming a psychologist. Not much time passed before he noticed Kelvin in the school cafeteria. Kelvin was nine years his junior, in his first year at university, and cute as a button. His wavy, dark brown hair, his bedroom eyes, and his striking profile reminded Rikki of the bust he had in his apartment of the Greek god Apollo. (Rikki later realized, however, that this judgment was largely influenced by the veil of his infatuation.) Rikki did not know if Kelvin was gay, nor did Kelvin know about Rikki's sexual orientation.

A few days later, while Kelvin was occupied with playing a pinball machine in the hallway outside the school cafeteria, Rikki seized the opportunity for an introduction.

Rikki, hesitantly, with a smile, started, "Hi. How are you?"

Kelvin responded, "Pretty good."

Rikki, careful not to extend his hand in greeting, so as not to interrupt Kelvin's pinball game, said, "I'm Rikki."

Kelvin smiled back. "I'm Kelvin."

Rikki, after a few awkward seconds of silence, commented, "You seem to be good at this game."

Kelvin said, "Yeah, I've got the highest score yet on this machine."

Rikki, noticing that Kelvin was beginning to lose his concentration as well as the game, said tactfully, "Let's meet at the bar when you're finished. I'll buy you a beer."

Kelvin replied, "Smashing. I'll see you in a couple of minutes."

Rikki walked to the bar that was located further up the hallway, a short distance from the cafeteria. He ordered a couple of pints and sat down, feeling both excited and anxious. His mind was racing. He had to think fast. What would they talk about? Just as Kelvin entered, a couple of minutes later, Rikki noticed a dartboard hanging on the wall at the back of the bar and said, as he turned to Kelvin with a smile, "Fancy a game of darts?"

Rikki didn't know how to play the game and discovered quickly that neither did Kelvin.

Kelvin, hesitantly, agreed. "Yes, that would be great."

The next hour was spent playing, not only one, but two games of darts. Kelvin, who was from Somerset in the southwest of England, spoke with the local accent and dialect. He'd say things like, "Ooh arr," which meant "Oh, yes." When Rikki managed to throw a dart anywhere in the vicinity of the dartboard, Kelvin would say, "proper job," which meant "well done." A couple of pints later and after a good chinwag (i.e., conversation), Rikki figured that it was time to get to know Kelvin more intimately and said, "Would you fancy coming into town and having a pint tomorrow evening?"

Kelvin answered, "Ooh arr, I'd love that."

Rikki continued, "Since I live in town, why don't you come over to my place and we'll walk from there."

Kelvin asked, "Where's it to?" (This meant, "where is it?" or "where do you live?)

After Rikki provided the address and gave him instructions on how to get there, Kelvin decided he would cycle into town from his dormitory and leave his bicycle at Rikki's apartment while they took in a few pints.

Kelvin arrived the following evening, and off they went to a pub across the road. There were more than three hundred and sixty five pups in the small city of York at that time—one for every day of the year—so finding a drinking hole was not a problem. As Rikki did not know if Kelvin was gay, he took him to a couple of pubs before ending the evening at the Yorkshire Arms, the only gay pub in town. As they sat there, Rikki asked in a hushed tone, "Do you notice anything unusual about the clientele in this pub?"

Kelvin, having noticed immediately when they entered that this was a gay establishment, said with a teasing smile, "Ooh arr. A lot of poofters here." (Meaning, of course, a lot of gays and lesbians.)

Until then, neither Rikki nor Kelvin had disclosed that he was gay. They liked one another, and neither wanted to sour the relationship, should the other be straight. And so they continued an intriguing evening of talk and laughter, while both managed to avoid talking about the "elephant in the room." After last call and a serving of fish & chips wrapped in newspaper and sprinkled with brown vinegar, and a side order of mushy peas, they made their way back to the apartment. Rikki invited Kelvin in for a nightcap. After a few drinks around the kitchen table, they confessed their secrets. One thing led to another, and Kelvin spent the night. As might have been predicted, over the succeeding days, a whirlwind of emotion let loose, as years of pent-up unrequited love gushed forward, never to be stifled again.

Kelvin had arranged for a week's holiday with his friends in Morocco prior to meeting Rikki, and, as the tickets had been purchased, he could not back out of it. So Rikki decided that this would be a good opportunity for him to go on a cycling tour in Scotland, which he had mapped out sometime earlier. After Kelvin had left, he took the train from York to Edinburgh and all the way to the little town of Thurso, situated on the north coast of Scotland. He then set out on his bicycle for a five-day cycle ride that took him along the north coast and down the west coast, toward Glasgow.

This was to be an enjoyable trip, but a new feeling had lodged itself in Rikki's heart. He was in love and the pangs of love weighed heavily. This feeling of heartache was new, a surprise, and not at all pleasant. It felt painful to be separated from Kelvin. He was distracted, and he could think of nothing else. He understood, for the first time, how it had affected him to shut the door on romance for so many years. The fear of being outed and ostracized had robbed him of this dizzying high, of being in love. This feeling wasn't entirely new, however. He had experienced similar feelings in the past toward some of his friends—but because none of them had loved him back, he never allowed himself to fall completely head over heels for them. Now he was head over heels, and the intensity was ten times stronger, ten times more wonderful—and ten times more painful.

As Rikki cycled up through mountain passes and down through beautiful valleys, he talked to himself aloud: *I never realized that being in love can bring such a feeling of freedom. No one could have described this to me before I had the courage to come out. I suppose it's like a caged animal that has never been allowed to run free, they don't miss it until after they have experienced the exhilaration.* Rikki continued this self-talk off and on throughout the trip, saying things like: *I hope every gay and lesbian will have this experience some time. All gays and lesbians have been robbed of this feeling by homophobic zealots. I will never ever be forced into the closet again. I feel great. I'm free, at last.* And, as the bicycle sped off the moor and down a gentle slope toward his final campground in the town of Ullapool, he sang the anthem: "Sing if you're glad to be gay, sing if you're happy that way . . . Hey . . . Sing if you're glad to be gay, sing if you're happy that way." [49]

---

[49]   Tom Robinson. Recorded by; The Tom Robinson Band, UK. 1978

Upon his return to England, Rikki was reunited with Kelvin, and he basked in the experience of being loved back for the first time ever. The emotional numbness that had built up over many years, on account of having concealed his romantic attractions, began to dissipate, as a dam gradually opened that exposed tender and vulnerable feelings, stifled since early puberty. It was 1981, the year Prince Charles and Princess Diana were married at St. Paul's Cathedral.

There was the issue of coming out to family and friends over the next few months, including to his mother, his father, and to his brothers and sister. His mother, who had separated from his father and moved to Canada shortly after Rikki had left for university, took the news well and only worried that he might be harassed or beaten up by thugs. His brothers and sister also took the news in stride. Rikki, however, worried that his father, who was remarried and still lived in Iceland, might take the news somewhat badly.

The following summer, Rikki decided that it was time to tell his father and that he should introduce him to Kelvin. A number of years had passed since he'd been home and since he had met with Old Soul at Heather Hill, and he longed for another meeting. There were many questions about life he wished to explore, especially the issue of sexual orientation and why Old Soul had been unwilling to give him advice in that regard when they last met.

That summer, Rikki and Kelvin set out on the express train from York to Edinburgh, and from there to the town of Thurso, where Rikki had visited on his cycling trip. A ferry took them from there on a two-day journey via the Faeroe Islands, to the east coast of Iceland. From there, they hitchhiked along the north and arrived at the farm of Lakjamot a couple of days later. Many years had passed since Rikki had last visited the farm, but, as usual, he was embraced with open arms and made welcome. After a hearty lunch, Rikki explained to Siggi that he wished to visit Old Soul at Heather Hill, as it had been ten years since they last met. Siggi replied jokingly, "I have not seen much activity on the slopes of

Heather Hill since you were here last, aside from a few sheep that graze there occasionally."

Rikki asked in return, "Do the sheep look spiritually inspired?"

Siggi chuckled. "No, but they sure provide for a good 'leg of lamb.'"

Siggi had plans to saddle a horse and inspect some sheep fences that afternoon that needed repair, and he offered to take Kelvin with him for the ride, while Rikki made his way over to Heather Hill for a visit with Old Soul.

On this occasion, Rikki decided to walk over to the fell, as his horse Trust had been felled some time ago, due to old age. He made his way up onto the large rock bed and, as before, walked in circles—thrice anti-clockwise and thrice clockwise—and then stood facing Heather Hill, this time thinking a loving thought about Old Soul, whom he had come to admire over the years. The doorway opened into the hill, and Old Soul invited him into his private study, as he had done on previous occasions.

After exchanging pleasantries and hearing about Rikki's travels, Old Soul knew that there was something bothering Rikki, and he said, "The last time we met, I was unable to give you advice about how you should deal with your sexual orientation."

Rikki replied, "Thank you, but I have, sort of, already worked through that without your help. It has been the most important issue in my life."

Rikki was surprised at the tone of his own voice as he blurted these words out, but Old Soul knew exactly how frustrated and hurt he had been on many occasions through the years about this issue.

Old Soul said, "Yes I know. You have done well on your own."

Rikki said, "I could have used your help."

Old Soul said, "Yes, but you had specifically stated that you did not want it."

Rikki was surprised. "What are you saying?"

Old Soul said, "You had specifically requested that I should not assist you, and stated that you would find your own way on that issue and I should not provide you with any comments that would ease your journey."

Rikki asked, "I did?"

Old Soul said, "Yes, we discussed this prior to your birth, and that is why I didn't offer any specific advice to you. Sorry, but my hands were tied."

Rikki, dumbfounded said, "We knew each other prior to my birth?"

Old Soul said, "Yes, of course. Remember what I said when we last met? You set in place all the major aspects of your life prior to birth, including meeting the people who will have a major impact on you. Although I am not exactly a person, I am one of them and so, for example, is your boyfriend, Kelvin."

Rikki said, "Oh, I see."

Old Soul said, "Last time we met, I was unable to tell you about your sexual orientation, but now I can. There is a good deal more to this than you know. As I've just said, there are certain fated events you placed in your path prior to birth. One of these was to create the conditions that would motivate you to leave Iceland and attend university abroad. If I had made you feel better about what you were going through when we last met, it would have changed your trajectory, and you would not have left Iceland. Also, you know now that in the late seventies and in the last couple of years, a disease called AIDS has begun to decimate the gay community. But because you were in the closet, you did not venture out into the gay community for sexual encounters, and you spared yourself this infection that has already killed so many. If I had supported you as a gay person and affirmed you in terms of your sexual orientation, you would have come out, and you would have contracted the HIV virus before it was known how it was transmitted. And you would now be infected with the HIV virus."

Rikki said, "Oh, I see. I think you have a point here."

Old Soul continued, "Now you can understand better why a lifetime is structured the way it is. There are multiple factors at play, involving the lives of a whole slew of people with whom you come into contact and whose lives are affected by your unique presence. If you had not left Iceland and if you were now infected with the virus, none of the individuals that you have met in the past ten years would have had the opportunity to be influenced by what your presence in their lives has provided. Of course, you would have met others here in Iceland, but your lifetime would have been truncated and not nearly as fulfilling and spiritually inspired as it has now become. That is why you requested, while planning this life, that I not provide you with any comfort in terms of the struggles you were having with regard to your sexual orientation."

Rikki said, "Thank you. I think you may have saved my life, or I may have saved it myself, before I was born! I see now how these sorts of things can only be understood in hindsight."

Old Soul said, "Yes, from your limited perspective. But from my vantage point, being outside the dimension of time, I can see what your future is likely going to be, depending on the decisions you make. And the consequences of major decisions, such as leaving Iceland and not coming out of the closet until now, are quite easy for me to see. But I will tell you more about that later."

Rikki felt sheepish. "I'm sorry for my indignant and angry outburst."

Old Soul; "No problem. I was well aware of how you were feeling before you came in today. Let me tell you a little bit about gender selection and sexual orientation, topics we did not discuss ten years ago."

Rikki answered, "Okay."

Old Soul continued, "You once commented that when I appear to you, I look androgynous. You are correct. I am an over-soul, and all over-souls are androgynous. You cannot tell if I look more male or more female; nor can you tell if I identify as either male or female. The reason for this is that there is no need for these delineations regarding gender in the spiritual dimension. On Earth, however, procreation is necessary, and the male body and the female body have evolved to meet the need for propagation of the species. For you as a soul, to incarnate in a male vs. a female body is, of course, a very different experience. And, because of the interesting social dynamics that exist between the sexes, there exist additional experiences, depending on what you've chosen to be, in terms of your identity.

You determine you gender, your masculine/feminine identity, and your sexual orientation.

"So, during gestation, one of the first things you do is to define the gender of the body. You also choose whether to identify as male or female. Most souls choose to align their identity with the gender of the body—a male identity in the male body, or a female identity in the female body. But not all souls choose this exact alignment, and there are several variations. At the opposite end of the spectrum you have a female identity in a male body or a male identity in a female body. This type of arrangement, which causes the person to be transgendered, provides for some unique opportunities in terms of experience during the incarnation. Manipulations of the physical body during gestation having to do with gender are also possible. For example, the soul may wish to feminize and alter the look of the male body by adding an additional X chromosome to the normal XY pair, causing the body to be what is called 'intersex.' So you see, numerous permutations are possible."

Rikki mused, "I see. I never realized . . ."

Old Soul continued, "After choosing your gender and your identity, you choose your romantic orientation—whether to be heterosexual or homosexual. Your gender, your identity, and your romantic orientation lay the basis for the most fundamental types of experiences you can anticipate during your lifetime.

"In this lifetime, you chose to have a male body, to identify as a male, and to be romantically attracted to the same sex."

Rikki replied, "Yes. But why do you call it a 'romantic' orientation rather than a 'sexual' orientation?"

Old Soul said, "I did this deliberately. Referring to a 'sexual' orientation rather than a 'romantic' orientation is a common misnomer that muddies the issue. When you use the term 'sexual,' there is an implicit reference that sex is the main determinant of the orientation—but it is not. It is the romantic fantasy and the loving attraction to the opposite sex—or to the same sex—that determines a person's orientation, not the act of having sex. It is what you think, not what you do, that makes you gay or straight."

Rikki replied, "Okay, I see."

Old Soul continued, "Of course, sex takes place in numerous situations, but it's most fulfilling for the individuals involved when it is used as a vehicle for the expression of love. But, as you know, that often isn't the case. People have sex for various reasons, including social obligations, a wish to have children, a wish to please themselves physiologically, a wish to please a partner or a spouse, or, in the case of the homosexual who's in the closet, out of fear of being outed and ostracized. Unless there is a genuine loving bond, fulfillment will always be limited in these circumstances for both partners.

"Now, let's get back to selection. Most souls choose not to make their sexual orientation an issue with which they have to struggle during their lives, and they elect to align their physical bodies with their male or female identity and to be heterosexual. There are also some who choose to be bisexual, which allows them to float between males and females as objects of romantic desire.

"You have chosen to be homosexual, which sets you at squares with prevailing societal norms in most communities, as they exist on Earth today. In some countries, you could end up in jail or face execution."

Rikki wondered, "Why did I choose such a difficult path?"

Old Soul answered, "It has to do with your soul's wish to experience specific feelings, as we talked about earlier. Planning your lifetime prior to birth is a serious business, and you spent a lot of time contemplating the decisions you made.

"Now, in terms of my specific advice to you, it is important that you embrace your sexual orientation. You chose to be gay. You did this for two reasons: One of your reasons had to do with your most recent past life that ended during World War II, as a Jew in Poland, which I mentioned to you the last time we met. During that lifetime, you were married with two children, all of whom died during a bombing raid. You survived the raid, and you were killed later, but you never overcame the grief of losing your family. This time around, you decided that the thought of having children would conjure up too many past memories of loss and, besides, you wished to focus on other issues. Your choice to be gay effectively steered you away from having children and to re-experiencing those intimate memories of loss."

Rikki nodded. "Yes, that makes a lot of sense to me."

Old Soul continued, "You also chose to be gay in order to have a depth of understanding for the necessary psychotherapeutic work, what lies ahead for you in terms of working with victims of the AIDS epidemic. AIDS will soon be killing thousands of gay men, and it will continue to kill millions of people all around the globe for some decades to come."

Rikki said sadly, "Oh, that is bad news."

Old Soul said, "It is an event that is fated on a societal level. You determine your own fate, as I told you earlier. But there is a lot more that is happening in the world. Your long-term goals must also be worked out within the confines of the evolving processes that take place on a societal level. If there is a conflict, then your goal will not be realized, or it will be modified so as to fit in within the overall unfolding harmony of events that are destined to take place, as all societies and all souls within them evolve spiritually. AIDS, while devastating, will create within cultures opportunities to evolve in numerous ways, not only in terms of morality and compassion, but also in terms of science."

Rikki's resentment toward Old Soul had dissipated by now. He felt a sense of calm and peace at hearing the support he had received with regard to his sexual orientation. He also realized that he would not have felt the resentment toward Old Soul on this issue if he had followed Old Soul's teachings in the first place and embraced his fate—accepting that he did not receive the information he wished for about his sexuality and trusting that he was meant to learn something from the experience. He now felt grateful, in hindsight, as meaning was bestowed on this event. He was thankful for having stayed in the closet, and he thought to himself, *Despite all my troubles to date, I would not change anything. I like who I am, who I've become.*

Old Soul, reading his thoughts, said, "Yes, you have done okay so far. Now remember to embrace fate, it is an easier path to follow."

Rikki agreed. "I see it now. Thank you. But before I forget, I meant to ask you about my supervising professors. Did I know the three of them prior to birth?"

Old Soul said, "Yes, you did. They are not part of your intimate circle of friends, but they agreed to help you out, should you come knocking at their doors."

Old Soul continued, "Now that we've explored the subject of gender selection and sexuality, I'd like to pick up on the topic of emotion I mentioned very briefly the last time we met."

Emotional States of Mind and Their Effect on Your Reality

Old Soul stood up and walked over to one of his bookcases. He pulled out a book, *Emotional States Of Mind*, and said, "I mentioned the last time we met how emotions play a part in creating reality. Now I'd like to tell you in more detail how this works from your personal perspective—how your interpretation of your own emotions creates your experience. The contents of this book will help you understand your own struggles with love, as well as with several other emotional states."

Rikki said, "Yes, that would be helpful."

Old Soul began to read passages from the book, taking time to discuss each passage, so as to ensure that Rikki thoroughly understood the contents.

Old Soul said, "I'll begin by reviewing some of what I said earlier, while adding some important details as I go along.

"As I've mentioned before, all over-souls and souls are highly intelligent thought forms. Their principal emotion is love. The opportunity to experience emotions, other than the serene experience associated with love, are limited within the spiritual dimension, and it is mainly for this reason that over-souls seek to project souls onto Earth for an incarnation. During the incarnation, souls, by way of having physical bodies, have the opportunity to experience the negative aspects of emotions that are not a normal part of life in the spiritual dimension.

"Love, which is a basic expression of the soul's nature, is fundamental to all types of emotion. It is experienced in mired forms on Earth, both through joy and in love for others, including love for animals and for other forms of life. Love is also experienced in 'emotional pain'. The intensity and depth of these painful emotions are often not realized fully until the object of one's love ceases to be, for example, due to death, or it is withdrawn, as in a relationship breakup.

"As I've mentioned earlier, during the course of your incarnation, you thrust yourself into circumstances that bring about emotion and then, as you slowly drift forward in life, you absorb all the potential learning from these encounters. The meaning of these encounters is not apparent to you at the time of the emotional upheaval, but is bestowed in hindsight, in other words, after you have learned what you intended from that particular emotional experience. In some instances, you will see meaning in events shortly after they occur, whereas at other times, it will not be evident to you until after many years—right up until your deathbed, or even following your physical death, when you have returned to the spiritual dimension."

> The soul's principal emotion is love, and love is the fundamental element of all emotion.

Rikki observed, "That seems like a long time to wait for meaning or for a meaningful understanding of the difficult times you have gone through."

Old Soul said, "Yes, but you will be surprised by how quickly a lifetime passes. Consider now, for example, how you just bestowed meaning on the event of me not giving you support about your sexual orientation when we last met: Ten years have passed in this instance. Usually, however, the insight whereby meaning is bestowed onto an event will not take that long, but in some instances it takes much longer."

Old Soul continued, "Now let's look briefly at the emotional states of love, fear, anxiety, anger, depression, and guilt, as well as the emotional state of persons who are absorbed with power. I know that you already have intimate experience with some of the examples I'll be telling you about, but it will serve you well to review these here, for sake of completion."

Rikki agreed. "Okay."

Old Soul continued, "Love is the most basic of these emotions, so let's look at it first."

Love

"As I just mentioned, the expression of love is a fundamental aspect of being human. People, however, will often run into trouble in their relationships with others when it comes to the expectations they have with regard to the love they expect to receive from them. This is certainly something you have already experienced on numerous occasions, when you attempted to seduce men in the past. Here are a few basics about some aspects of love you should understand.

"It is important for you to know that love is 'unidirectional.' Love only flows from yourself to another person or to someone you intend. When it is directed to another person, that person may sense your love and bathe in its essence. Your love, however, is not reflected back to you. However, the other person may feel similarly to you and direct his or her love to you, allowing you to bathe in a similar emotion, but it is not 'your' love that is reflected. So, remember, do not feel upset when someone doesn't love you

back when you love him. It is a flawed assumption that love will be reflected back, given that love is unidirectional."

Rikki said, "Oh, I guess that explains a few things."

Old Soul smiled knowingly and continued, "It is also important that you understand that *love is 'unconditional.'* That is to say, you should never expect anything in return for loving someone or for being kind to them. Love and kindness are gifts that are to be given freely. Expecting that these acts or feelings should be returned is a flawed assumption, given that love and kindness are unconditional. So to reiterate this principle: You need to understand that an act of love or an act of kindness you offer someone is not freely given if you expect something from that person in return. This twisted expectation is quite common and frequently leads to confusion by the recipient and disappointment by the giver. If you expect something in return for your love or for an act of kindness, be it solicited or unsolicited, then voice your expectation, for instance, 'I will be expecting something in return from you' or 'now you owe me one!' In this instance, you are doing someone a favor, and although it may be motivated by your love or kind feelings for them, your favor is an aside from these feelings and it is conditional; it is not a direct act of love or kindness, it is a favor. Also, in this type of instance, don't expect that the recipient will be able to read your mind and that he will return your favor unsolicited, as you might have done for him, or for her. It may not occur to him, and you do not have a right to resent him for that. In this instance, the motto 'ask and you shall receive' aptly applies."

Rikki understood this well and mentioned his friend Bjorn to Old Soul, commenting, "Bjorn has a very dysfunctional relationship with his mother. He often comes over and hangs out for long periods of time. I think his mother's love for him is a good example of what clearly is not unconditional. There are strings attached to every affectionate gesture she makes toward him, all of which are unsolicited and unwanted. She whines and says things like, 'After all I have done for you, is this all I get in return,' 'disrespect,' 'you bastard.' Bjorn is a product of a one-night stand she had with a man who wanted nothing to do with his mother afterward, but she continued to live with him for a couple of years, in an abusive relationship."

Old Soul said, "Yes, this is a good example. I'll comment on the abuse later, however. Let me continue with some basic aspects of love."

Old Soul continued, *"Love cannot be demanded.* You cannot demand of someone else that they love you, and neither can you force yourself to love someone you don't love, no matter how hard you may try. Your love for others and theirs for you, either 'is' or 'is not.' There is not much you can do about changing that.

"Another common twisted expression of love that occurs in relationships is that of jealousy. *Jealousy* is the fear of losing the loving affection of someone you love to someone else. It may lead to extreme emotional pain. It is a feeling of utter dread, and it's characterized by an insatiable desire to prevent a lover from turning his or her romantic affections away and focusing them onto someone else. The jealous person, in an attempt to regain the affection of the person who has turned away, may resort to attempts to dominate, or show ownership, over their spouse. At this point in a relationship, however, fear has set in, and love ceases to find its natural expression; the relationship becomes void of love. Always try to avoid these twisted emotions where love becomes entangled with jealousy and dominance. These are insidious and frequently develop when romantic relationships begin to deteriorate."

Love is: unidirectional, unconditional, it cannot be demanded, and it is subjective.

Rikki said, "I think I have had a few inklings of this feeling of jealousy over the years."

Old Soul said, "Yes, I know."

Old Soul continued, "You must also understand that *love is a subjective experience,* and its occurrence emanates from a history of personal experience that is, of course, different for every human being. If you had the opportunity to step inside your lover's body and to experience the world as it is seen through his eyes, you would discover, much to your amazement, that his love for you is often premised on entirely different assumptions than your love for him. For example, your love may, in part, be a reflection of your need for companionship, whereas his love for you may reflect his need for security. Generally, however, love in romantic relationships is transcendental and based on motivations that are largely unconscious to both people."

Rikki said, "Yes, I have difficulty putting my finger on exactly what it is about Kelvin I love."

Old Soul said, "Love is a complicated affair.

"The need to be liked and the 10 percent rule apply," Old Soul continued. "Closely related to love is the need to be liked by others and to have close friends. Young people, especially, find it difficult to accept when they discover that everyone doesn't like them."

Rikki said, "I want to be liked by everyone, well, by most people anyways."

Old Soul said, "It's not possible to be liked by everyone, and I'll explain why. I remind you of the fact that you are unique. There are several billion people currently on the planet, and not a single one is identical to you. The differences between people are so vast that it is illogical to expect that most of them would like you, or for that matter, that you would like them. I would say to you that if you have one or two 'best friends,' then you are rich in friendships.

"A good rule of thumb to keep in mind with regard to your wish to be liked is what I call the 10 percent rule. I suggest that if you expect to relate well to more than one in ten people you meet, or if you expect that more than 10 percent of everyone you meet would want to seek you out as a friend, then you are deluded."

Rikki said, "Okay. As I think about it, I realize that what you are saying is probably correct. In fact, I doubt if I 'click' with more than 10 percent of everyone I meet. But I still wish that everyone would like me."

Old Soul said, "Well, that just does not happen. On average, 10 percent will like you, 80 percent don't care who you are, and 10 percent won't like you—even before you open your mouth."

Rikki sighed. "Yes, I suppose you are right. I feel about the same way toward others I meet, if I am to be honest about it."

Old Soul said, "I suspect that if you were to ask your friends and acquaintances about this, you would discover that many of them suffer from this delusion. It is not uncommon for people to assume that 30 percent or even 50 percent of the people they meet will like them enough so as to want to form a friendship with them.

"Being deluded in this way usually doesn't become a problem for most people, but for some it does. Unfortunately, for some people, the wish to be liked becomes an obsession, and a lot of time and energy are wasted in trying to achieve this unattainable goal. This pursuit is invariably self-defeating, and it takes on many forms. A person, for example, in an attempt to achieve this goal may study someone he or she seeks to attract and attempt to act 'as if' they are the type of person they predict that person would like them to be. In so doing, they, of course, sacrifice their own needs in their desperation to be liked or to be loved. The problem that occurs is that this desperate pursuit becomes a way of being for some people. In the extreme instance, they forget who they are. They forget that they are unique. They only think about their partner's needs, wants, and desires, and they lose the connection they have with their own. These people invariably suffer from low self-worth and gradually, as they forget who they are, they find it increasingly difficult to let go of their need to be loved for fear that no one will like them, or love them. They adorn a mask, and in so doing, violate the basic premise for their existence—which is to be themselves unapologetically. This game, that is for the most part unconscious, takes many twists and turns and always ends up in grief when the individuals involved get to know each other more intimately and discover that they are not compatible."

Remember the 10 percent rule and be yourself unapologetically.

Rikki said, "I've known a few people like this. It's almost as if they are in a trance."

Old Soul said, "Yes, you are right. You remember we talked a little bit about trance states when we last met. The stronger the emotion, the deeper the trance. Or in this example, the stronger the desperation to be liked or to be loved, the more anxious a person feels, worrying about being unlovable. It is very difficult for a person to break out of this habit, and it becomes an obsession, at times."

Old Soul continued, "On the other side of the coin, with regard to this type of social interaction, when a person is true to himself and expresses himself unapologetically, his friends come to know him authentically. He is authentic to himself and to his friends. They, in turn, react to him accordingly, and the feedback he gets from them reminds him of who he knows himself to be. This feedback, or echo, from other people reinforces his identity; his sense of who he is, or his sense of self. This confirmation, reflected from the outside world, is extremely important for psychological stability. When a person adorns a mask and pretends to be someone different, then the echo he receives from others does not align with his inner identity, and he naturally concludes that his friends do not know him, which in fact they don't. The absence of this confirmation of self from the outside world makes a person feel increasingly isolated. He begins to feel alone, even when surrounded by friends. And if this behavior is prolonged, he may begin to experience panic attacks. For this reason, you must always obey the first principle of your existence, which, as I've said before, is to be yourself, unapologetically."

Old Soul concluded, "Now try to keep these few comments about 'love' and your wish to be 'liked' in mind, as you encounter situations that bring about these feelings, and you will avoid a great deal of unnecessary strife in your relationships with others."

Rikki said, "Okay, I will."

Old Soul continued, "As I said earlier, the joyful experience of love is the only emotion you normally experience in the spiritual dimension. The negative sides of love that occur in relationships, such as the ones we have discussed above, where you experience emotional pain, only occur in the physical world. And as you well know, there is emotional pain associated with numerous other emotional states as well. These include, for example, fear, anxiety, anger, depression, guilt, and power. Understanding a little better how you interpret these emotions when you experience them will be helpful, as it is also through them that your experience of reality is created. Let's look at these in turn."

Fear and Anxiety

"Fear and anxiety are primary emotions. They arise from separate sources: Fear is an emotion that occurs when a person perceives a threat, and it emanates from the 'basic consciousness' inherent within the physical body. It is an instinctual survival mechanism and serves to protect the body from physical harm and the consequent experience of physical pain. Anxiety, on the other hand, is associated more with 'existential' aspects of life, and it emanates from the soul consciousness."

Rikki asked, "What do you mean?"

Old Soul said, "Do you recall the last time we met, when I talked about how you are a combination of two types of consciousness—the 'basic consciousness' of the physical body and the more sophisticated consciousness of the soul?"

Rikki said, "Yes, I remember."

Old Soul said, "Good. Fear emanates from the basic consciousness. It is primal. All animals, including the human animal, experience fear when they feel threatened, and it elicits a 'flight' reaction or a 'fight' reaction if the animal is cornered and cannot flee. Anxiety, on the other hand, emanates from the consciousness of the soul and has to do with the trepidations about living in the physical world. There are basically two types of anxiety—common, everyday anxiety and existential anxiety."

Rikki said, "Okay, I understand."

A thought-stopping technique helps alleviate anxious obsessive thoughts.

Old Soul continued, "Let me first tell you about the common everyday type of anxiety. This type of anxiety is usually associated with situations that are imagined and temporary or situations that are anticipated. Anxiety of this sort is always a waste of energy. It achieves nothing, and it usually annoys your friends when you tell them about it, especially when you make no attempt to resolve it despite their advice."

Rikki commented, "I know someone like that. She obsesses and complains about her ex-boyfriend, but she never takes my advice about what I think she should do in order to feel better about the situation."

Old Soul said, "My general advice would be in these types of situations—if you can solve a problem, then act and make the choices required to solve it. If you can't solve it, then don't think about it. Let it go."

Rikki said, "That may be good advice, but it is easier said than done. It's not easy to just stop feeling anxious, for example, about a romantic relationship that is on the rocks."

Old Soul said, "Yes, I know. There are therapeutic techniques that will help a person gain control in those sorts of situations."

Rikki asked, "Do you have a recommendation?"

Old Soul said, "You have read about the 'thought-stopping' technique that I am about to describe, but let me review it for you anyway, as it is extremely effective if applied properly. It focuses on helping a person let go of an anxious thought and, consequently, an anxious feeling—since a thought always precedes a feeling. The first thing people must understand is that they are in control of what they allow themselves to think about. You—and no one else—decide what thoughts you allow to be in your mind. This thought stopping-technique will help you to force an unwanted thought out of your mind, permanently.

"First, clearly identify the obsessive thought you are attempting to get rid of. Define it and write it down. It must be specific. It might, for example, be a specific ex-lover you can't get out of your mind, a specific event, or an incident that upsets you and that you can't stop thinking about.

"Next, make an executive decision in your mind that you are ready to let go of the unwanted thought. Let's use the ex-lover in our example. In this instance, you must be absolutely certain that you are ready to stop obsessing about him. Once you are certain that you have made this decision, continue to step three.

"Now, every time the unwanted thought pops up into your mind, you say to yourself *Stop,* in an attempt to push the unwanted thought out. To help you with this task, you will need to concentrate on a distracting task, something that occupies your mind so that you cannot at the same time think the unwanted thought that you are training yourself to get rid of. So, as an example, when the thought of your ex pops up in your mind, say, '*Stop*' and then engage in one of the following distraction tasks: count backward by three's from one hundred, as quickly as you can; do the alphabet backward, or every-other letter of the alphabet backward; or calculate square-roots of numbers. Any mental task will do, as long as it preoccupies you to the extent that you cannot at the same time entertain the unwanted thought in your mind.

"Continue to do the distraction task in your mind until you have a sense that the unwanted thought has disappeared.

"This may take a few minutes when you first attempt this, but trust me, it will work; the unwanted thought will eventually vanish.

"Once you have a sense that the unwanted thought has been pushed out of your mind, focus your mind on some activity that is necessary for you to do and that occupies your mind. In your instance, for example, you should sit down and work on your schoolwork."

Rikki said, "This sounds like it might work."

Old Soul said, "Yes, it will. But a few words of caution, before I finish. In the beginning, during the first few days after you start doing this thought-stopping technique, you must be very vigilant, as the unwanted thought will creep back, and it will suddenly be in your mind without you having noticed. When this happens you must immediately say to yourself, 'Stop' and then resume your distraction task until the unwanted thought has vanished again. Don't be disillusioned when you first start using this technique, as it may take a number of minutes for the unwanted thought to vanish the first few times you try this, but if you are disciplined, and the success of this technique depends solely on you being very disciplined with yourself, you will soon discover that you are no longer plagued by the unwanted thought. A final recommendation: In some instances, you may not be fully ready to let go of the unwanted thought prior to commencing this mind purge. If that is the case, then I suggest that you schedule into your diary a time, no more than once per week and no longer than ten minutes at a time, when you allow yourself to think about the unwanted thought, in other words, your ex, in our example. Before you do this, set an alarm clock to ring after ten minutes. Then sit down with pen and paper and write all of your thoughts and concerns you have about your ex. When the alarm goes off, say to yourself, '*Stop,*' and commence the distraction task until you have extinguished the unwanted thought. If you have not finished thinking about all the unwanted thoughts when the alarm goes off, then make the same schedule the following week. Remember, you are training yourself to take control over what you think about, as opposed to having unwanted thoughts control you. This final recommendation will allow for you to deal with any leftover issues you may have about your ex, but on your own terms and under your own control."

Rikki nodded. "This is good. I'll recommend it to my friend the next time she talks about her former boyfriend. It sounds like this would work for any person who is obsessively infatuated with someone who isn't interested, or for anyone who is obsessive about anything."

Old Soul said, "Yes, it is a good general technique."

Old Soul continued, "Now that we have explored common everyday anxiety, let me tell you a little bit about 'existential' anxiety. Like common, everyday anxiety, existential anxiety also has to do with trepidations the soul experiences during an incarnation. But it is more closely associated with purpose and meaning in life. Existential anxiety can occur in a variety of circumstances. It, for example, is not an uncommon experience for persons who are very unhappy in their careers. When they lack fulfillment and worry about their purpose in life, they feel melancholy and often begin to experience panic attacks and typically feel anxious and depressed, especially on Sundays, while dreading having to go into work on Monday. Another example would be a student like yourself who flunked in school. Suddenly, the future is uncertain, and existential anxiety sets in."

Set long-term goals to help alleviate existential anxiety.

Rikki said, "Yes, this is this the type of feeling I experienced when I received the report card saying that I had flunked my entire year in high school and that I would have to repeat it. I had a panic attack. I couldn't control the anxiety and the shame I felt in that moment. And I had a similar experience after the first semester at university, when I failed every one of my courses except psychology."

Old Soul said, "Yes. You experienced brief episodes of existential anxiety at those times. It's a very uncomfortable emotion, and it usually motivates a person to make choices that will lead to some significant life changes. As an example, in your case, you immediately began to formulate a different trajectory in terms of your education, which has led to your current career. The good news is that in these types of circumstances, as soon as a positive action is taken, the symptoms of existential anxiety begin to subside. On both occasions, when this happened to you, you quickly decided on new long-term goals and began to work toward new destinations. These goals allowed you to set your sails and to steer your boat with a purpose toward a goal you had in sight. In this way you, in effect, pulled yourself forward, out of a circumstance that caused you to experience the existential fear."

Rikki said, "Yes, I can see that now."

Old Soul continued, "There is, however, a more serious form of existential anxiety than what you have experienced. As you know, your over-soul continuous to exist in the spiritual dimension during your incarnation, while your soul, your inner identity, and your outer ego dwell in and around your physical body. Occasionally, however, when a person experiences extreme anxiety or is severely traumatized, the outer ego and the inner identity stop functioning properly; they become broken and cause a disruption in communication to the soul. In some instances this disruption continues for very long periods of time. In these situations, a person may experience post-traumatic stress disorder, which is a severe form of existential anxiety associated with deep emotional pain. This condition usually requires psychotherapeutic intervention."

Rikki said, "I don't think I've experienced that type of existential anxiety."

Old Soul said, "No, fortunately you haven't."

Old Soul continued, "Now let's continue exploring other types of emotion. As I said earlier, love, which is a basic expression of the soul's nature, is a fundamental element of all emotion. Fear and anxiety are primary emotions, but they often give rise to secondary emotions. Anger, depression, and guilt are examples of secondary emotions. Let's begin by looking at anger."

Anger

"Anger is a secondary emotion arising from fear and anxiety," Old Soul went on. "It often occurs when a person feels threatened and is fearful of something. The most common obstacle that gives rise to anger has to do with a person's relationship with the space/time dimension. You may remember that I talked a little bit about this during our last meeting?"

Rikki said, "Yes. You talked about how frustrating it is for souls to adjust to the space/time dimension when they attempt to navigate and communicate using a physical body."

Old Soul said, "Yes, and they often become angry. Common instances that give rise to anger are, for example, being stuck in traffic, waiting for someone who is late for an appointment, or not having the time to complete something important. These types of examples, where space and time play a central role in the ability to achieve a goal, are the most frequent causes for frustration and anger."

Rikki said, "Yes, I understand. I tried to practice what you had said a few years ago, but I still become impatient in these types of situations, although it happens much less often now, as compared with before you first told me about this."

Old Soul said, "That's good. I saw you practice this concept on a few occasions with your friend Alfred. Buddhist monks are good examples of persons who have mastered this art, but you don't have to practice meditation or be a monk in order to be good at this. But you are correct in discovering that it does require a lot of practice and continued mindfulness for a soul not to become frustrated and angry while attempting to navigate within the space/time dimension. There is a truth to the saying 'patience is a virtue,' as it quells this type of anger."

Old Soul continued, "Fate is also woven into this mix, as well as the unfolding harmony of events into which you were thrown at birth. Fate dictates that there are unexpected events around every turn. Some of these have to do specifically with your own personal fate, but others are simply part of the general obstacle course in life brought about by the unfolding harmony of events. It might be helpful for you to use the analogy of yourself floating down a river in a boat and not knowing the location of the rocks below the surface that suddenly cause the boat to tumble and disrupt your journey. Or you can imagine yourself standing still, while the wind that blows toward you brings with it unforeseen events. These events, whether fated specifically to appeal to you or simply a part of the general obstacle course of life, need to be negotiated. It is the attitude you take to these obstacles that creates anger. Your attempts to hurry faster through space/time than the river flows, or your impatience at the wind when it is still, will only serve to make you frustrated and angry. You cannot be outside space/time, or escape it; you have no choice but to accept it and to work within its confines."

Continued mindfulness is needed while navigating within the space/time dimension.

Rikki nodded. "Yes, I'll need more practice to achieve perfect serenity." Old Soul continued, "There are, of course, many other sources of anger. For example, anger might occur in the wake of the disappointment you feel when you discover that someone has lied to you or when someone breaks a promise. The anger in these instances is caused by disappointment. At a deeper level, this anger often relates to the feeling of not being liked or of not being loved. Anger is also common when relationships break up, where the emotional pain of losing a lover leads to fears of abandonment and of not being likable or of not being lovable.

"Another common source of anger is the twisted expectations some people have after providing solicited or unsolicited favors to another person, when they mistakenly assume them to be acts of love and kindness. I talked about this earlier in the context of unconditional love or unconditional kindness. But let me elaborate on this a little further, as it also relates to anger. In some instances a giver continues to dish out favors, while none are ever returned. In this instance, he slowly begins to feel that he is being taken advantage of and that he is sacrificing himself for nothing. He begins to feel hurt, then angry. His anger builds up, and he begins to become resentful and irritable with others. Eventually, he blows his lid, sometimes at the unsuspecting individual who is receiving his favors, but more commonly at a person with whom he is close, or at some unsuspecting person who just happened to be in the wrong place at the wrong time. Or, he may also turn this anger onto himself, inward, in which case he begins to feel depressed."

Rikki said, "I think I know someone like that—my friend Cindy. It was difficult to spot at first, but now that you have explained this, it fits her to a T. She works with me at my part-time job at the coffee shop during the school year. She pretends to be happy, but I can tell that she is angry, inside. She is always talking about how nice she has been to others, what she has done for them, how helpful she is, and how she hardly ever receives any acknowledgement in return for her help. I suppose I should look out; maybe she'll suddenly blow some steam off at me?"

Old Soul said, "Yes, she may. It sounds like she incubates her anger and it builds up."

Old Soul continued, "Anger sometimes leads to more extreme feelings, such as revenge. I mentioned revenge the last time we met, when I advised you of how important it is to embrace fate in order not to become vengeful. When a person is obsessed with revenge, he has lost the connection of love that exists between his own soul and the souls of others. He mistakenly expects to find peace in the aftermath of taking revenge. The colloquial sayings 'two wrongs don't make a right' and 'violence begets violence' have evolved out of the discovery that human suffering does not heal through revenge. The reason for this is that all souls have in common the fundamental emotion of love, and, on a higher spiritual level, they are all connected. It is as if they are all fingers on the same hand; if pain is inflicted on one finger, it is felt by the entire hand. This is the reason why revenge never quells emotional pain; on a spiritual level, you are merely re-injuring yourself."

Revenge never quells emotional pain.

Rikki said, "I see. I understand better, now, as the examples pile up, what you meant when you said that I should embrace fate. That idea seems to come up again and again in different contexts."

Old Soul said, "Good, you are making the connections."

Rikki asked, "But what about people who talk about needing revenge in the form of justice, in order to find closure to a dreadful event that someone perpetrated against them?"

Old Soul said, "There is nothing wrong with finding closure through the process of justice. However, if that person requires the death of another human being in order to find justice, then closure for him will prove to be elusive, as the death of one never justifies the death of another. Closure is about healing from grief, not an eye for an eye. Lovingly embrace your fate. Your challenge is to learn from the emotional experience that is created in grief, and, in time, to transcend that experience."

Rikki said, "Yes I agree, but embracing fate is not the first thing most people think about when a member of their family has, for example, been murdered."

Old Soul said, "I know. This is a very hard spiritual lesson. But like all fate, it is orchestrated by yourself in order for you to have the opportunity to learn about your inner nature.

"Now let me tell you a little bit about depression. Depression is also a secondary emotion, but unlike anger that expresses the consequences of fear and anxiety outward, depression expresses fear and anxiety inward."

Depression

"As you know, depression is accompanied by feelings of hopelessness, pessimism, impending doom, despair, and in extreme cases, feelings of suicide," Old Soul continued. "In the severely depressed person, the outer ego has ceased to function, and the inner identity is in a shambles. The connection with the physical world is lost, and the person becomes disconnected from life: His sense of belonging is severed, along with his longing for existence; he has lost the emotional connectedness to life around him, and he feels emotionally numb. He does not feel joy, and he is not able to identify with the joy he sees in others; he feels no compassion. He is, in fact, disconnected from life. He has fallen below the horizon from which emotions are felt. He may know that there is a horizon somewhere far away, but he is unable to get there on his own. However, when the depression begins to lift, glimpses of the horizon begin to come into view—first sporadically and then with increasing frequency."

Rikki was listening thoughtfully.

Old Soul continued, "As you know, the events in life that cause a person to feel depressed are numerous and heartfelt, but it is an experience that the soul has elected to have, in order to learn about its inner nature. Why, you ask. The answer lies in the concept of contrast that we discussed the last time we met. You cannot appreciate the heights of joy and the experience of bliss unless you are able to contrast these elevated mood states with their opposites, such as depression. Metaphorically, you cannot appreciate the exhilarating beauty of standing on a mountaintop unless you have toiled in the valley. You do not know how good a sunny day feels unless you have experienced feeling gloomy on a cloudy day. And the list goes on. In order to judge an experience, you must be able to contrast it with an opposite. It's obviously not a pleasant experience to be depressed, but it is an emotion you must experience in order to know the opposite."

Rikki asked, "Are you saying that depression is unavoidable, and that I am bound to experience being depressed sometime in my life?"

Old Soul said, "It is a normal part of life to experience the ups and downs as you negotiate through the fated events that appear in your path. It is not necessary however for you to experience clinical depression in every lifetime, as you may have had sufficient experience with depression in other lifetimes you've had in the past, in which case there may be no need to experience it again this time around. It is also possible that you have plans to be clinically depressed in a future life."

Rikki said, "Okay, that is a relief—I think."

Old Soul continued, "In terms of experiencing both sides of the coin, you may also recall that I mentioned a similar concept with regard to the divine dichotomy the last time we met. In that instance a person is forced to experience who he is *not*, in order to have a better understanding of who he *is*. That predicament will, of course, often lead to feelings of depression, as the person becomes undone and collapses emotionally."

Rikki said, "Yes, I can see how that would happen."

Old Soul said, "As with all encounters that lead to emotions, you are thrust into a circumstance that brings about that emotional state within you. Once the emotion is sufficiently felt, you slowly begin to drift forward, absorbing all the potential learning from that encounter. In some instances, however, with depression, especially when the depressed state has been deep, your outer ego will need a push or a pull to overcome the inertia and to start operating again. There is always a danger of settling into depression for such a long period of time that it becomes a lifestyle or a miserable habit."

Rikki wondered, "You mean, a person continues to be depressed when the circumstances that led to the depression have long since passed?"

Old Soul said, "Yes. People sometimes become trapped. Some individuals discover, once they are depressed, that there are secondary gains in being depressed. The emotion then settles in for the long term, and the depressed mood may become an aspect of their personality. If you ever notice that this is happening, than make an attempt to visualize yourself at the top of a mountain and see yourself struggling up the slope from down below. Ask yourself, 'What is the best advice I can give myself in order to get up and climb out of this mess I am in?' Remember, you created the events that led to your depressed state; and you must get yourself out of it, unless, of course, you wish to stay! You have free will, and the choice is always yours. Most people benefit from psychotherapy and sometimes from psychopharmacological assistance as well, when they find themselves in this circumstance, to restart their outer ego and overcome the inertia caused by the depression."

Rikki said, "You just said, 'you created the depression, now get yourself out of it.' Would that not sound a little harsh to a person who is feeling depressed?"

Old Soul said, "Yes, it would, but sometimes harsh words will help a person for whom depression has become a habit; help him to overcome the inertia and begin to consider other options. You may remember what I said the last time we met, about emotions being interwoven with trance states. A depressed person is also in a trance, and the trance is instrumental in sustaining his depression. A kick in the pants might jolt him out of the trance."

A depressed person is also in a trance.

Rikki, hesitantly, said, "I see. I don't think I've ever been depressed, in the way you just described it."

Old Soul said, "No, but you have experienced some symptoms of depression from time to time."

Rikki, reflecting on his past, remembered, "It always took me some time to recover from my infatuations."

Old Soul said, "Yes. Infatuations are a good example. The trance is very prevalent when you are infatuated."

Rikki said, "Yes, I felt I was in a trance."

Old Soul said, "You were mildly depressed during those times, as are many young people when they wrestle with the tumultuous emotions they feel the first few times they experience unrequited love."

Old Soul continued, "One of the problems with depression is that the soul of the chronically depressed person has a very limited ability to express itself into the physical world, due to the fact that the outer ego has failed, and it is no longer absorbing information. The soul's communication with the physical world is therefore blocked. When this condition persists for long periods of time, the soul and, consequently, the over-soul, are no longer able to experience new learning from the incarnation. The purpose for the lifetime is therefore negated. The ultimate response to such a condition may be the outer ego's wish to self-destruct, possibly via suicide, as it feels it has become useless. It reasons incorrectly, along with the inner identity, whose communication with the soul has also been damaged due to the depression, that they have become useless and obsolete."

Rikki said, "That doesn't sound good."

In suicide, you flunk life.

Old Soul said, "The problem is with the outer ego that is damaged, but it is never damaged beyond repair. The outer ego of the suicidal person may not wish to admit it, but it always has numerous options when it comes to choosing between life and death. With suicide, you forgo the opportunity to learn anything further from the emotional experience of being depressed and from the eventual recovery from the depression. You, in effect, 'flunk' life. And this is a waste in instances where the body is otherwise physically healthy. This may sound insensitive, as I know there are times when the emotional pain is seemingly unbearable and the depressed person cannot accept for a moment that he or she has elected to feel this way. But keep in mind, your soul will never set you up for a situation it knows you ultimately cannot handle. There is always a way forward. There is never a night so dark that light does not follow on the morrow."

Although the world is very full of suffering,
It is also full of the overcoming of it.

- *Helen Keller*

Old Soul continued, "In some instances of prolonged depression there may be other motivations at play. Remember, the soul invited the circumstances that led to the depression, and it may wish to prolong the depression, for example, in order to provide the depressed person's family and his caregivers with the experience of looking after someone who is chronically depressed. However, the ultimate meaning, the reasons that a person's depressed mood refuses to budge, may not be known to him or to his caregivers until after his passing."

Rikki, reflecting on what Old Soul had said about depression, commented, "My friend Bjorn's mother tried to kill herself a couple of years ago. She took an overdose of pills. But he decided to skip school that same day, and he arrived home unexpectedly to find her unconscious on the living-room sofa, and he called the ambulance. I suppose she was surprised when she realized that her time to die had not arrived."

Old Soul said, "You are right, death is never an accident, but most people do not have the information beforehand, as to when they will die. However, there are many complicated factors to consider in the circumstances of your friend's mother. For one, she has a history which she does not wish to confront. The experience of having survived near death, however, provided her with a new perspective on life and a willingness to confront some of her demons. Bjorn's life was also forever changed as a consequence of having discovered that his mother had elected to die, rather than to see him grow up. Having saved his mother from the brink of death, however, also caused him to re-evaluate his relationship with her—which he needed to do. As you can see, life is a complicated affair! There are no simple answers."

Rikki said, "Yes, I understand that."

Old Soul continued, "Now I'd like to tell you about the state of mind that occurs when you experience guilt."

Guilt

Old Soul continued, "Guilt is an affective state of mind in which one experiences emotional conflict at having done something that one believes one should not have done (or conversely, having not done something one believes one should have done). Guilt usually lingers and does not go away easily. There are basically two types of guilt you need to be aware of. There is *true guilt and false guilt.* An instance of true guilt might, for example, occur after a premeditated crime, where a person knew

When you feel the pangs of guilt, remember to determine: Is it true guilt or false guilt you are suffering?

beforehand that the act that he was about to commit was wrong, but he nevertheless carried it out. Afterward, he suffers true guilt, and he may at some point want to atone for his deed, in the hope that he may be forgiven. False guilt, on the other hand, is a feeling that arises as a consequence of a false core belief, usually relating to the space/time dimension."

Rikki, stepped in, and commented, "Again, the space/time predicament complicates matters."

Old Soul said, "It is the most common stumbling block that souls must contend with.

"An example of this would be the common accusation: 'You should have known better'—when, in fact, you could not have known beforehand. Or a denunciation about something that was impossible for you to have known beforehand. As with the occurrence of anger that we discussed above, false guilt is directly related to the fact that a person is not sufficiently alert to the fact that he is trapped in the space/time dimension and, therefore, he cannot know what will happen next. As an example, you may accuse yourself and say, 'If I had known that would happen, then I would not have done it' or 'If I had been there on time, then this would not have happened.' The list is endless.

"It is, of course, illogical and absurd in instances such as these to blame oneself, yet your society conditions you to do so, suggesting that 'you should have known what would happen.' Of course, if you had known, then you would have acted differently. People routinely make these types of accusations, despite knowing that it is impossible for anyone to know what will happen next. In these circumstances, I ask that you: remind yourself of the fact that nobody on Earth knows what is going to happen next and recognize that your only responsibility is simply to do the best you can, in every circumstance. You should also keep in mind that your 'best' will vary depending on the circumstances you find yourself in. You may, for example, be tired, fatigued, distracted, deep in thought, or otherwise absentminded at different times, which will cause your level of performance to very. To do your best is all that you can ask of yourself, and indeed of anyone else. It is all anyone can do. At the end of the day, as you fall asleep, simply remind yourself that you did your best, given the circumstances. Then let it go. (Of course, if you intended to screw up and you succeeded, than you either feel no guilt or suffer true guilt. But you would definitely not suffer from false guilt). Remember, *to suffer from false guilt is an error in understanding that is based on a false core belief about the space/time dimension.*"

Rikki said, "This certainly sounds familiar. I am especially reminded of an incident that happened to me while at school, many years ago. The instructor had spent some time teaching us how to make calculations on the slide rule. I was pretty good at it—until he asked me to come up and demonstrate my skill to the class. I got nervous standing up in front of my peers, became confused, and forgot in the moment how to do it. The teacher was furious and yelled, 'Why are you so stupid? You know how to do this.' I felt dreadfully humiliated and terribly guilty as I wandered in a daze back to my seat. I did my best, but my nerves got the best of me. I felt guilty afterward. I suppose it was false guilt?"

Old Soul said, "Yes, this is a good example, and I'm sure you can think of many more that have happened since then."

Old Soul continued, "Another common pursuit that often leads to false guilt is the striving to be 'perfect.' Again, this is based on a false core belief about the space/time dimension. In your culture, the directive to try to be perfect is drummed into children by well-meaning parents and teachers who are attempting to motivate you. You, therefore, and naturally, assume that 'perfection' is something that is attainable. You discover, however, that you will never succeed at attaining perfection. You feel bad when you do not meet your own expectations and guilty that you do not perform up to the standards set for you by your elders. As time goes on, repeated failures begin to undermine your confidence, and you become hesitant in your efforts, as you discover that true perfection is elusive.

"It is important for you to understand that there is no such thing as perfection. The notion is based on a false core belief. You can never expect to be perfect, as perfection means a state of fulfillment beyond which there is no future growth, and no such state exists. What you may consider to be perfect in one moment will not be perfect in the next. Your own judgments and other people's judgments, along with everything else in the physical world, change from one moment to the next, on all levels, as the entire universe slowly breathes in and out, as is reflected in the unfolding harmony of events as they come into existence and disappear. Don't worry about perfection; it's unattainable. *The idea that you can achieve perfection or that you can be perfect is a false core belief. It can never be achieved. Let it go.*"

> A happy person is not a person in a certain set of circumstances;
>
> But rather a person with a certain set of attitudes.
>
> *- Hugh Downs*

> Always do your best and know that perfection does not exist.

Rikki said, "I know I can never by perfect, but must I be so imperfect?"

Old Soul said, "The more you scrutinize yourself—your body, your performances, or your memory—the more you judge yourself to be wanting. This is a universal truth. You may remember, the last time we met, I told you not to judge yourself."

Rikki said, "Yes, you were telling me about being unapologetic for my existence."

Old Soul said, "Yes, your attention should not be focused on yourself. You should focus away from yourself and into the physical world around you. Bring your eyes to focus on what you are doing in the world, not onto your navel. The body and your mind are meant to function without your conscious attention being focused on them. In school, you have learned about the body's autonomic nervous system, and you know, for example, that your heart beats without you having to think about it. Your digestion takes place without the need for your conscious attention focused on it. However, if you begin to focus your attention on these autonomic processes, you bring them into conscious awareness, and they cease to function as effectively.

Focus off your navel and into to world around you.

"The same is true for self-judgment. In your society, young people almost always judge themselves to be wanting in one way or another. Do not judge yourself. Leave it to others to formulate their opinions of you. All you are required to do is look through your eyes into the world—away from your body—and be yourself unapologetically. Focusing your attention onto yourself and obsessing about how well you are doing mentally or how well your body is functioning physically only serves to disrupt a process that is meant to be automatic. A good example of this is in the act of sexual performance; the more you focus on how your penis is functioning, the less well it will do. It may go limp or you may not reach orgasm. Focus away from your body and onto the object you desire, and your body will look after itself and function splendidly."[50]

Rikki said, "I like that. I'll stop navel gazing."

Old Soul said, "Good. Now a few words about power through domination."

Power

Old Soul continued, "While power through domination isn't an emotion per se, I will mention it here, as it is a state of mind that

---

[50] For more information on this therapeutic concept of 'de-reflection' see Victor E. Frankl. *The Will To Meaning: Foundations And Applications Of Logotherapy.* New York: Penguin Books, 1969.

is also secondary to fear and anxiety: It has to do with the fear of losing affection and love from others.

"Power through domination is common in romantic relationships and also in relationships at a person's place of work. In all instances, it is an act motivated by the fear of not being loved, of not being liked, of being abandoned, of being unwanted, or of being unloved. Power through domination, however, invariably has the exact opposite effect to what was intended. It alienates both the dominator and the person he or she dominates, as their feelings of love and kindness become blocked and cannot find expression. When this happens, the dominator gradually begins to experience existential anxiety, and he responds by exerting more power in the relationship in the hope that he will be loved again, but it never works."

Rikki said, "My friend Bjorn once told me that his mother was physically abused by his father. He dominated her through intimidation and aggression for a couple of years, until one day she had the courage to leave. I suppose that situation fits with what you are describing?"

Old Soul said, "Yes, that is a good example: spousal abuse and what has been termed the 'battered wife syndrome.' The confidence and self-worth of the battered spouse is so depleted that they often do not have the courage to leave, even when the door is open for them to go."

Old Soul continued, "Power through domination is an insidious process, and it occurs at all levels of society—from the dictator right down into the bedroom."

Rikki said, "I've read about the abuse of power happening in many countries all around the world."

Old Soul said, "Yes, but be careful not to confuse power through domination with leadership, status, or honor, which are attributes bestowed onto a person by his or her peers. What often happens, however, in terms of leadership, is that leadership gets twisted up with the pursuit for power. This is most typical in the political arena, when a leader becomes fearful that his designation will be withdrawn. As his fear increases, he begins to exert power through domination over his subjects. This usually occurs in the context of believing that he is in competition with his opponents for a moral high ground on some particular issues. But, as is true in personal relationships, on a societal level, power through domination invariably has the opposite effect from what is intended. The love and kindness the subjects had for their leader becomes blocked and does not find expression, and the leader feels increasingly alienated and unloved. Existential anxiety begins to set in, and the leader gradually turns into a dictator, as he responds by exerting more and more power in the hope that he will once again experience the love he once received from his subjects, but it never works. *Remember, the pursuit of power through domination is an expression of existential anxiety and mistakenly assumes that love can be demanded."*

Old Soul now paused in his delivery, and said, "We have discussed different emotions today and the effect they have in shaping your reality. But before we conclude, I'd like to pull together some of what I've said about how the soul learns about its inner nature and add a couple of points about the process of how this inner learning takes place.

Rikki agreed, "Okay."

Learning About Your Inner Nature

Old Soul said, "I have mentioned on numerous occasions that souls create the circumstances that bring about the opportunity for them to create emotions. This, in turn, provides them with the opportunity to discover something about their inner nature and to evolve spiritually. In that regard, I spoke about several topics: How souls prepare and set the stage for an upcoming incarnation; how the soul determines its own fate both before and during the incarnation; and how, in numerous circumstances, 'free will' is a double-edged sword where you may choose to be who you are not, be forced to be who you are not, or choose to hurt yourself and others close to you in order to discover who you are. I also spoke about how learning about your inner nature takes place through the experience of love, fear, anxiety, anger, depression, guilt, and power.

"But there is one additional process through which 'inner learning' takes place that I haven't described to you yet."

Rikki was curious. "What's that?" he asked.

Old Soul continued, "Let me first give you a little background on how 'emotional memories' are stored. As I've just said, you create the circumstances that bring about the situations from which you create your emotions. Once the emotions are created, you store them in your mind as emotional memories, along with the associated thoughts that produced them and the timeframe for when they occurred. But the cataloging, or grouping together, of the different emotional memories, is, first and foremost, according to their association with one another. A secondary cataloging takes place according to the specific thought that generated the specific emotion, and a tertiary cataloging is made according to the time the emotional event took place. So what you end up having are groupings of similar emotions that are stored by 'emotional association,' or by analogy, in specific 'drawers in your dresser.' As an example, all emotional experiences that deal with betrayal are stored in one drawer. Another drawer will contain all the emotional experiences of abandonment, and a third will contain abuse, a fourth, fear of the dark, and so on."

Rikki said, "Okay, I understand."

Old Soul continued, "There is also a bleed-through between the drawers. As an example, memories of betrayal recalled from one drawer will trigger related memories of abandonment in a different drawer, and so forth.

"Because of the way the cataloging of these emotions takes place, it becomes very difficult to search through your drawers for a specific thought that produced a specific emotion, and it is virtually impossible to know the exact historical timeframe for when an emotion associated with a particular type of event first took place."

Rikki nodded, and said, "Okay, I understand."

Old Soul went on, "Now, this is the important part of the explanation I want to get to.

"What happens occasionally is that the thoughts and the associated emotions you generate in your mind shock you, and you find them to be extremely distasteful. You can't understand how a 'good' person like yourself could have such despicable thoughts, and you hate yourself for having them.

"When this occurs, your impulse is to shut them away and not to deal with them. What you should know, however, is that these types of experiences are normal. Every person has them occasionally. Your 'outer ego' and your 'inner identity' are immensely creative, and they cause you to think of all sorts of things, including the unspeakable. It is normal for you to massage, toss around, and analyze every situation you encounter from all possible angles, as part of your inner experience and inner learning. So, for example, when you read about a sexual assault in the newspaper, your imagination may take you to how it would feel to be the injured victim, how it would feel to be the perpetrator, how it would feel to be a close family member, etc. If you are unable to resolve your feelings about the situation in your waking life, you continue to work on them through your dreams and nightmares, until you arrive at a peaceful understanding.

"But, occasionally, when these thoughts and emotions are just too much for you to handle, you resist thinking about them altogether, and you lock them away securely in the back of a drawer where you hope they will never see the light of day. The problem is that, over time, the drawer fills up, right to the brim. And when that happens, the stuff you've refused to look at begins to weigh on you, as those thoughts and emotions cry out to be heard. In extreme cases, they surface in the form of what might be described as 'episodes of extremely uncharacteristic behavior,' and you will usually remember these episodes quite well afterward. And in other extremely rare instances, these rejected thoughts and emotions express themselves through a multiple personality, where another discrete personality forms out of these unresolved emotional issues."[51]

Rikki commented, "That would be disturbing."

Old Soul agreed. "Yes, it would be. But fortunately that happens very rarely. What you should know is that sorting through these unwanted thoughts and emotions is one of the main roads to learning about your inner nature. They, along with the socially acceptable thoughts and emotions that you accept, define who you are, no matter whether you like it or not. They are a vital part of you, and that is why they are virtually impossible to ignore for an entire lifetime. As they cry out for a voice and for understanding, they cause you to become triggered by seemingly innocuous events that occur in your daily life. When that happens, all the emotions contained within the same drawer come to the surface at once, and you see yourself overreacting in a situation. That is why it is important for you to take time and sort through your drawers—deal with what's troubling you—from time to time. The more you are able to do this during the course of your lifetime, the more content you will be."

Rikki asked, "Are you saying that everyone should go for therapy?"

---

[51]   For further reading on this subject see; Adam Crabtree. *Multiple Man: Explorations in Possession and Multiple Personality.* Toronto: Somerville House, 1997.

Old Soul replied, "Most individuals would benefit from having an opportunity to talk to a professional sometime during their lifetime. But that may not be their fate. They may have decided that to struggle with their unwanted emotions for their entire lifetime will provide for a more interesting, albeit more difficult, learning experience, through which they will eventually find meaning as a consequence of their suffering, either on their deathbed or following their death. That is, of course, also why you cannot force someone to have therapy. They have to be prepared for it, and they must want it. And it must also be something they fated for themselves."

Rikki said, "I suppose that's where the saying comes from: 'You can lead a horse to water, but you can't make him drink.'"

Old Soul said, "Yes. You must wish to change before any change is possible."

Rikki, hesitantly, asked, "What types of unresolved issues do I have in my dresser of drawers?"

Old Soul answered him, "One issue, which is now resolved, occurred when it dawned on you that you were gay. Of course, as I've said earlier, it was your choice to be gay, but the important part of your inner learning was how you faced this challenge. How would you come to terms with your inner nature in the context of the prevailing prejudice that existed within your country? You did not want to be different in this way at first, and it took a few years for you to come to terms with it. Fortunately, you never experienced self-loathing or disgust at your feelings. You had free will, and you accepted these same-sex attractions as an aspect of your nature, but with the caveat not to tell anyone and to clamp down on your romantic feelings until you felt it was safe to come out. The critical point I want to make here is that there is always a choice. You set this situation up as a challenge to yourself, and this is how you responded."

Rikki nodded. "Yes, that is correct."

Old Soul continued, "Of course, no two situations are exactly the same, and others make different choices based on a variety of factors. For some, discovering their same-sex attractions elicits feelings of disgust and self-criticism—and in some instances, it leads to self-destruction. These individuals are unable to meet the challenge they set for themselves and turn their negative feelings onto themselves. Teenage suicide attempts and suicides are, unfortunately, common in these circumstances."

Rikki said soberly, "I was fortunate. I never felt suicidal."

Old Soul said, "No, the circumstances that you fated relating to this issue were less dire than many have set for themselves. For example, you had intimate friends, you had grown used to being different on account of your stammer and dyslexia, you were not effeminate, you were not singled out by your peers and scorned, and you did not grow up in an oppressive religious household or with parents you thought would disown you if they knew.

"While some turn their feelings of disgust inward, others turn them outward, in the form of hatred toward homosexuals. Some of these individuals are consciously aware of their homosexual attractions, whereas others are not. In their desperation, they torment others for what they are unable to accept in themselves. It's a sad state of affairs, as they have not met their own challenge. Some of these individuals are gay-bashers."

Rikki said, "Yes, I know someone who admitted to me that he was a 'gay-basher' before he was able to come to terms with being gay. He felt really bad for what he had done."

Old Soul said, "Yes, as I mentioned earlier, sometimes a person must cause a lot of pain to himself and to others before inner learning can take place."

Old Soul continued, "A similar situation takes place with other types of bullying. Teenagers are especially vulnerable to torments of this sort from others, because they have a stronger need for acceptance by their peers, and they have not yet developed a sufficient sense of independence. The bullies, in these instances, see in someone else a vulnerability they themselves have not been able to cope with. Their hatred stems from their own inability to deal with what they perceive to be the same shortcomings in their victims' character."

Rikki commented, "I know that bullying sometimes happened at school when I was young. It never happened to me, but I once bullied someone I hardly knew at all. It was a kid a year older than me who lived at the end of our street. My friends and I, for reasons I cannot remember, decided that he was a bully and, in retaliation, made the trip over to his house on a couple of occasions and yelled outside, 'Karl is a bully, Karl is a bully.' Years later, I ran into him, and he told me how tormented and isolated we had made him feel during this time of his youth. I still feel awful about what we did."

Old Soul said, "It is good that you feel remorse. You were having difficulties accepting aspects of your own character at that time, and you projected them onto him. As I've said, sometimes you have to be who you are not, in order to discover who you are.

"Milder forms of emotion stemming from these types of unresolved issues happen frequently in daily life, and you can identify them quite easily. They are always associated with a gut reaction to something that has just happened, and you surprise yourself with your own reaction, which is just a tad too extreme. It could be anything—even something very insignificant on the surface, such as someone's outfit or manner of speech. But it triggers related, unresolved emotional memories that have been stuffed into your drawer, and they all float to the surface at once, causing your reaction."

Rikki said, "Yes, I have a reaction like that sometimes. It's complicated. I usually can't figure out why I have them."

Old Soul said, "Yes, I know. You experience an emotion, but the memories and thoughts associated with that emotion, which might help you to understand why you are experiencing it, are not readily available. And the time-frame for where they might have originated is even more difficult to discern. If you are particularly troubled by these types of emotional reactions, then a few trips to the therapist's office would give you an opportunity to peek into your dresser and open the drawer that contains the associated unresolved emotional memories.

"Don't, however, confuse this type of visceral reaction with having a strong and a valid opinion about something. That is normal and a part of who you are; your uniqueness, warts and all, which you must be unapologetic about. Yet it is healthy to question your own opinions and behavior when they are not in accordance with the highest ideal of who you hold yourself to be. At the other extreme, however, too much navel gazing or self-reflection is unhealthy. It will make you neurotic, and you will begin to question every move you make when you stop looking away from your body and into the outside world with both eyes."

Rikki asked, "What do you mean 'with both eyes'?"

Old Soul explained, "When one eye is looking at your navel, analyzing your every reaction, and the other is looking into the world around you, you are distracted and question what you are doing. If this continues, both eyes may become drawn to your navel and your relationship to the outside world becomes interrupted, at which time you have violated the most basic premise of your existence, which is to be yourself unapologetically and to thrust yourself into the world."

Rikki said, "I see. It all ties together. You also warned me about the perils of naval gazing when you spoke about perfection, earlier."

Old Soul smiled. "Yes. It's easy to lose sight of the importance of looking out into the world around you, when you become bogged down with the nuances of life."

By now, Rikki had received a lot of information, and he needed to digest it. Old Soul was aware of this, and, preparing to bring the visit to a close, he said, "Well, that's all I have for you, for the time being. We have covered a lot of information today. Do you have any questions you'd like to ask of me?"

Rikki, reflecting on everything Old Soul had told him, commented, "You seem to have such a grand view of everything that is happening in this world. How does that happen?"

The Grand Theater

Old Soul said, "It's one of my hobbies. The dramatic theatre of life on Earth is always fascinating for me to watch. For me, it's like when you sit down and watch a soap opera on TV. Here in the spiritual dimension, I turn on my TV and watch your physical world. I can tune in and see your life—and anyone else's—unfold in a grand soap opera as if I were looking through your eyes, with your unique take on the world. Then I can switch channels and watch your friends' unique perspectives, as they see life through their own eyes, and so on, for every individual. In addition to turning my attention from one individual to another—as you would a dial on a radio, in order to pick up different stations that are being broadcast simultaneously—I can also 'tune' to channels that allow me to view aspects of the unfolding harmony, as it strings events out over time. In this way, I can see entire soap operas as they unfold between members of a particular family, between relatives and friends, extended families, and up the ladder to dramas unfolding between ethnic groups, cultures, nations, and the entire world. You see, there is a grand unfolding harmony among all these levels and among all events that take place on every level. I can see all these layers of events as they coalesce to form the river of life as it unfolds on Earth.

"Of course, by being outside the space/time dimension, I can also 'fast forward' and see what is likely to happen in the future—and I can 'rewind' and see how events in the past have layered one upon another to form the history that has taken place on Earth. I cannot know your exact future, but I can see in broad terms, knowing the confines of the physical world and your free will within it, how your lifetime will unfold, depending on the choices you make. Minor decisions you make during the course of your day will not alter your life, but the probable trajectories your life will take based on major decisions and the long-term goals you set are more interesting for me, and I take time to view them, especially in so far as you are concerned. And as your theatrical drama comes to a close at the end of your lifetime, you will return home to the spiritual dimension and sit here where I am sitting, and watch life's dramas unfold as I do now, until one day you decide to jump into one of these dramas again, in order to learn something new about your inner nature, during the course of another lifetime."

Rikki said, "That is awesome. It makes perfect sense, when you explain it in this way."

Old Soul stood up and said, "You now have the basic information that you will need in order to thrive in life. Over the next few months, and indeed over the next few years, you will gradually integrate this information more thoroughly as you encounter day-to-day circumstances that will illustrate why it is important for you to be mindful of these basic concepts."

Rikki stood up, thanked Old Soul, and turned to leave. As on previous occasions, he felt as if he were sucked through a porthole back into the Earth dimension. No time had passed, as was the case on previous occasions. His wristwatch showed the exact time as when he had entered the hill. Rikki sat down and took in the view, looking over the Shrub Valley River and far into the distance at some mountains on the horizon. The air was unusually still. The land was full of energy and activity. A gentle breeze swept by and he enjoyed the wafts of fresh air filled with the smells of heather and artic flowers. The birds could be heard chirping among the heather, while others fluttered about. The experience was breathtaking, and Rikki felt privileged to be alive as he began his walk back to the farm.

On his way back to the farm, Rikki realized that, through his meetings with Old Soul, he now had a near complete theoretical framework of the processes that take place in order for a soul to have a lifetime on Earth. There was much to think about. Today's lesson on emotion built on what he had learned previously and provided a glimpse into the nature of emotions and how best to cope with them when they occur.

He thought to himself: *Old Soul's towering view of the universe and of us mortals living down here on Earth is something else. I'll look forward to sitting next to him someday. Then again, I'll probably want to come back down here and live another lifetime. I love it here. It's nice to know that I'm able to come back as often as I please. No need to accomplish everything in this life, I suppose!*

When Rikki arrived at the farm, Kelvin and Siggi had already returned from an afternoon spent repairing some sheep fences. As they sat down for afternoon coffee, all ears were on Rikki for tidings from Old Soul.

Kelvin, tired and sore from having spent a couple of hours on horseback for the first time, commented, "My legs aren't used to being stretched like this. I don't think I'll ever walk again."

Siggi, jokingly, said to him, "I'll fetch the wheelbarrow for you when you stand up from the table."

Kelvin asked, "What happened at Heather Hill? Did you see Old Soul?"

Rikki, feeling a little overwhelmed after an intense day, smiled hesitantly and said, "We talked about a lot of things, and I learned a lot, but I'll have to sleep on it before I'm ready to tell you all about it."

Rikki remained rather quiet throughout afternoon tea. Sometime later that same day, Rikki and Kelvin made their way to Reykjavik, where Rikki's father greeted them with open arms. His father had heard through the grapevine a few months earlier that Rikki was gay, and he had found it difficult to accept at first, but after discussing the matter with his wife, who was familiar with the homosexual lifestyle, he was able to accept the situation.

A couple of weeks later, Rikki and Kelvin returned to England, where they both resumed their studies at university. Rikki, in his spare time, was employed at a local psychiatric hospital where he trained psychiatric interns in the techniques of group psychotherapy. These were good times. A lot of evenings were spent at local pubs drinking pints of beer and conversing with fellow students. Hot servings of fish & chips, wrapped in newspaper, sprinkled with brown vinegar, and accompanied by a side order of mushy peas became the norm on the walk home from the pub. Rikki was in love and living with a boyfriend for the first time in his life.

The city of York is steeped in culture, and the oldest section is fortressed by a Roman stone wall that encircles most of the old city. Ghost sightings in old buildings are common, and an entire Roman Legion was once seen walking through the basement walls of the York Minster, by a worker doing repairs. There are numerous walkways along old cobblestone roads that are dimly lit. That autumn, during the year following John Lennon's death, female students walking on their own in the early evening along forested lanes began to be clobbered over the head by someone who sneaked up from behind and dragged them off into the bushes. Fear settled over the university campus, and female students began to wear bicycle helmets on their walks home. Peter Sutcliffe, known as the Yorkshire Ripper, was arrested a couple of months later, in January 1981, and convicted of having killed thirteen women and having left seven others for dead after attacking them. The fear among female students, however, continued, as there was a widely held belief that the Yorkshire Ripper had an accomplice who was never caught.

Rikki often pondered what Old Soul had said about there being no accidental deaths. Did John Lennon, as well as these women, choose to be murdered? It was difficult to fathom this aspect of

Old Soul's spiritual existentialism. The assumption was logical from a spiritual perspective, in the context of what Old Soul had said about souls needing to create emotional experiences to learn about their inner natures. From down here, in the physical world, though, it was incomprehensible to accept that anyone would wish for such an ending. Surely there must be other, less violent, ways to create the emotional experiences required for a soul to evolve? Then again, murders have taken place throughout the ages, and in wars, large numbers of people are slaughtered in equally brutal ways.

Rikki and Kelvin were well suited for one another, and their relationship was good for the first few years. They completed their degrees; Rikki began to work as a psychologist in the prison services, while Kelvin pursued a post-graduate degree as a dietician. Kelvin's studies, however, required frequent separations due to student/study placements that took him to numerous areas of England for weeks on end. These separations became marked by heartache, tears, and painful separations at the train station, which put a strain on their relationship. Kelvin, eventually, grew tired of his studies, and, after completing his degree, decided to retire from that profession.

The grass looked greener across the pond, and, as Rikki had taken out Canadian citizenship before leaving for England, he had an opportunity to return to Canada. They decided to move. This decision, however, demanded another heartfelt separation, compounded by the fact that Kelvin had to stay with his father, who was dying of cancer. The separation lasted for an entire year, and, aside from phone conversations, Rikki could not be present for Kelvin during these sad times. The stress on the relationship began to cause some fractures in their intimacy. They agreed to have an open relationship during this separation, although neither of them frequently availed themselves of this provision.

Kelvin eventually arrived in Canada, following his father's death and after obtaining immigrant status. They made earnest attempts at homemaking—a new home and three dogs became part of the family. But the relationship did not survive these upheavals. A couple of years later, after unsuccessful attempts at closing the open relationship status, broken trust and sexual jealousy began to fester as the flame of love gradually grew dimmer and eventually burned out. The relationship had lasted eight years. It was a fairy-tale romance that fell victim to the proverbial seven-year itch. However, after a brief separation, Rikki and Kelvin were reacquainted and began a lifelong friendship.

Rikki never returned to visit Old Soul at Heather Hill, but he often thought of him and the guidance he had provided. The spiritual philosophy of a dual existence—one on Earth and another within the spiritual dimension—seemed to extend the reach of life. Death was merely an end to a journey that you designed in order to learn about your own inner nature and to evolve spiritually.

Knowing you had willfully entered life in order to learn something about yourself gave life a purpose. Your existence wasn't a random event, and you weren't placed on Earth against your will. You actually envisioned, studied, and prepared for this opportunity. Having the vantage point of being outside of this dimension and the ability to see the flow of life on Earth allowed you to make some general plans about how your lifetime would unfold before you embarked on the journey. Once you set off, you had free will to strive for whatever you desired, within the confines of those boundaries you had set. And you were able to make course corrections along the way and set fated events in your path that would ensure that you met your goals. Your only responsibility was to thrust your uniqueness into the world and to be unapologetic for your existence. Everything else would flow from there.

Old Soul had given Rikki some general ideas about how all of this took place and of how we experience the physical world while looking into it by means of our physical bodies, and how we create our experiences through a fluid interaction of our soul's uniqueness, trance states, emotions, goals, free will, fate, and core beliefs, that together shape our experience throughout our lives. This spiritual/existential framework for human existence became the platform for Rikki's psychotherapeutic approach, as he worked for a number of years in health-related institutions and later with victims of the AIDS epidemic, as Old Soul had predicted. He excelled in his private practice, where he specialized in past-life and life-between-life regression techniques, as Old Soul had also predicted he would do.

Chapter 6

Epilogue

M ANY YEARS PASSED, AND on one sunny afternoon, while walking his dog, Rikki was struck by a car. The force of the impact tossed his body up over the roof of the vehicle before it tumbled onto the pavement behind, head first. At the moment of impact, his consciousness vacated his body, and Old Soul suddenly appeared. As Rikki levitated above his body, fully aware, he thought to himself:[52]

Whew. What just happened?

Old Soul, standing next to him, read his thoughts and said, "You were thrown out of your body."

Rikki asked, "Where is my dog?"

Old Soul said, "He's fine, he ran off to the side just before the car hit you."

Rikki, still reeling from this strange experience following the impact, said, "That's good." And he continued, "This is strange. I feel more alive and alert now than when I was in my body."

Old Soul said, "Bodies are always experienced as a drag on the soul, due to the lower vibrational levels within the physical world. It may surprise you to know that leaving your body at the time of death is actually much less traumatic than entering the fetus during gestation."

Rikki asked, "Am I dead? I mean, is my body dead?"

Old Soul said, "No, your body is in a coma. You have not died yet."

---

[52] For extensive research in this field of enquiry, please see: Pim Van Lommel. *Consciousness Beyond Life*. New York: Harper Collins, 2010. Also; Michael Newton. *Destiny Of Souls*. St. Paul: Llewellyn Publications, 2000.

An ambulance arrived a few minutes later, and Rikki's body was transported to the hospital, unconscious, having suffered a severe concussion. Old Soul accompanied him in the ambulance, and, as he lay there, Rikki continued to levitate a few inches above his body.

Rikki said, "I don't' feel any pain. I like this feeling. It's like I'm floating through the air."

Old Soul said, "Well you *are* floating."

The ambulance pulled up to the hospital, and Rikki was rushed in on a gurney and transported to the emergency room on the second floor. Monitoring instruments of all sorts were gathered and hooked up to his body, as well as an intravenous drip. The nurse, after searching through his wallet, found his ID and called his husband, John. They had been married for a number of years.

Old Soul said, "Let's see how severely your body is injured."

Rikki, looking down at his body, observed, "Oh. It does not look good. Look at it—it's a mess. All that swelling on my face. I look awful."

Old Soul, anticipating the next few minutes, said, "Let's go for a walk. It's about to get distracting here when John arrives."

Rikki agreed. "Okay. Good idea. I know my body looks pretty bad, but I feel fine. Where am I? Is this the spiritual dimension?"

Old Soul said, "No, you are in the same space that ghosts and other discarnate spirits reside. You are still on the Earth plane, but slightly out of alignment with that dimension."

Rikki said, "Oh. I remember you telling me about spirit entities many years ago. Am I a ghost?"

Old Soul said, "Yes, in a manner of speaking, but your body is still alive. The type of conscious awareness you are experiencing right now is temporary."

Rikki asked, "What am I to do?"

Old Soul said, "There is nothing to be done right now. Let's walk around the hospital grounds and have a look at what we see."

Rikki and Old Soul floated down the hospital corridor and into the main lobby, where John, accompanied by a friend, had just arrived.

Rikki, looking at John, said, "Hi, Johnny. Sorry about the accident. Don't worry, I'm okay."

John signed in on the ledger at the front desk and proceeded to walk right through him, on his way to the emergency room.

Rikki said, wonderingly, "He walked right through me?"

Old Soul asked, "What did you expect? You only have your astral body. You are invisible to the human eye."

Rikki said, "Yes. Sorry, I forgot."

Old Soul said, "Let's go outside."

As they floated out and around toward the back of the hospital, Rikki commented on a few ghostly figures that were sitting on a bench. "Look at those ghosts sitting over on that bench."

Old Soul said, "These are the ethereal bodies of individuals like yourself. Their bodies are also in a coma. They are waiting to see what will happen next."

Rikki, looking ahead said, "Oh, my goodness, I see my mother."

Rikki's mother had passed away a few decades earlier from breast cancer. She looked radiant and much younger than she had at her death at the age of sixty-three. They embraced warmly.

Rikki asked, "How have you been? I've missed you."

Mother said, "My afterlife has been wonderful. You know the sun always shines back home in the spiritual dimension."

Rikki said, "You have come to guide me back, haven't you?"

Mother answered, "Not until you are ready."

Rikki said, "Let me introduce you to Old Soul."

Mother, winking knowingly at Old Soul said, "It was fortunate that you were able to be with Rikki at the time of the accident."

Old Soul smiled. "Well, you know, I'm never far away."

Rikki suggested, "Let's go and see how my body is doing."

As they floated up into the emergency room, they saw John sitting at his bedside, holding his hand. He had been crying and looked exhausted.

Rikki commented, "I'm having difficulty feeling the sadness he's experiencing."

Old Soul said, "Now you understand a little better why we incarnate on Earth. We are unable to experience these types of emotions in the spiritual dimension. The only way to learn about them and the effect they have is to have a physical body and to create them through experiences on Earth. Once this has been done, however, you can always revisit a past life and relive the emotion with full effect, and study the details of every experience you ever had during that lifetime. It's like the hollow deck in Star Trek. Once a program for a particular lifetime is activated, you can step into it at any time during that lifetime and experience it as if you were there again. In this way, you are able to re-experience every emotion, while at the same time, you can understand fully what you were attempting to learn about yourself when you created it."

Rikki said, "Yes, I can see that more clearly now."

Old Soul said, "Now you can also see why you have had so many incarnations on Earth. In every incarnation, you focus on a different aspect. It's like building up a DVD collection that you can view later. You design your lives in order to experience every possible emotion. The possible emotional experiences are virtually endless, depending on the culture you incarnate into, your gender, education, and income level, etc., as well as what role you and your friends have decided to play during the incarnation."

Rikki asked, "Do I always incarnate together with my friends?"

Old Soul said, "Yes, for the most part. You have a large group of friends in the spiritual dimension, and prior to each incarnation, you discuss the details of what your objectives will be for each incarnation and what role you will play in each other's lives. For example, you may be a parent to one of your friends in one lifetime and then switch roles in the next life and be that person's child. Or you may take turns at upsetting or physically harming one another during successive lifetimes, in order to discover the emotional consequences of that type of experience."

Rikki said, "I like that. I remember you once told me a little bit about this when you were telling me about depression—how everyone needs to have different emotional experiences in order to evolve spiritually."

Old Soul said, "Yes, you continue in this way, through successive incarnations, until you have exhausted all the experiences you wish to have."

Rikki said, "I remember you saying that I once had a lifetime as a peasant in Iceland around 900 AD, a North American Indian in the eighteen hundreds, a mentally delayed child in the seventeen hundreds, and a Polish Jew in the thirties."

Old Soul said, "Yes, and there have been many more. Once you have had all the experiences you wish to have, you will have evolved sufficiently to ascend to a higher tier in the spiritual dimension, where different experiences become available to you."

Rikki asked, "What other types of experiences?"

Old Soul said, "These are endless. You may, for example, sit on a council of elders, where you help souls evaluate their experiences shortly after they have returned from an incarnation on Earth. You may work as a guide or a fylgja to souls who are incarnating, as I have done with you. You may work at rescuing lost souls, or soul fragments, that have not found their way back following their incarnations. You may work at assisting souls with preparation prior to their next incarnation. You may work in the initial guidance and nursing of newborn over-souls as they first develop in other non-physical dimensions, before they attempt to incarnate on Earth. You may work in the design of new worlds and in the design of new life forms, in other dimensions. The list is endless."

Rikki said, wonderingly, "I never imagined."

Mother, looking at Rikki's body, said, "Rikki your body looks like it will remain in a coma for some time. It looks quite damaged. You are also likely to have suffered brain damage when you hit your head."

Rikki said, "That doesn't sound good. I wonder if I'd be mentally delayed if I were to recover enough and survive this accident?"

Old Soul, watching his words so as not to influence Rikki's decision, said, "It is likely that you will have some mental difficulties."

Rikki said, "I already had a short life in the past where I was mentally delayed. I don't think I'm ready for another one, especially since, as you once pointed out, I have not worked through all my issues from that lifetime as of yet."

Old Soul said, "This would be different. You would retain your intelligence, but your brain would not work properly. You would have difficulty speaking, and your body would be paralyzed on the right side. It's definitely a learning opportunity, if you would like to have that experience for a few years."

Rikki said, "I don't know what I should do. I know Johnny has better things to do for the rest of his days than to look after me."

Old Soul said to Mother, "Why don't you take him home and see if the council of elders is available. They would be able to help us out in this situation."

Mother said to Rikki, "Okay. Take my hand, and I'll lead you through into the light."

In that instant, Rikki and his mother began to ascend up into the sky as an invisible force pulled them upward.

Rikki, looking around, said, "I can see the entire city and the surrounding countryside from up here."

Mother said, "Look up."

Rikki said, "I see a bright light."

In that instant, a beautiful, serene light enveloped them. Rikki felt an ecstasy of exhilaration and anticipation. There seemed to be a presence up ahead, but he could not make it out. The force continued to propel them at lightning speed, until suddenly, they slowed down and drifted in a dark space filled with what appeared to be both large and small clusters of brightly lit orbs, as far as the eye could see.

Mother said, "Well, here we are. Welcome home."

Rikki said, "This reminds me of inside Heather Hill, when I visited Old Soul."

Mother said, "Yes, this is the spiritual universe. Does it seem familiar to you yet?"

Rikki said, "I have a feeling I've been here before."

Mother said, "Your memories will soon be restored. See the cluster of orbs up ahead? Will yourself toward them. There are some friends waiting for you to arrive. I have a few things to attend to, and I will meet up with you later."

Rikki had seen this space before inside Heather Hill, when he sat in Old Soul's study. But this time, he was able to propel himself, or will himself, forward in among what appeared to be little villages of orbs. As he drifted onward and drew closer to the cluster of lights up ahead, he suddenly found himself in a large hall, standing in front of a long table with five individuals sitting behind it. Old Soul had already arrived at the hall and stood behind him, slightly to his left. Rikki recognized immediately that this was the council of elders, and he knew that they had been expecting him. They were dressed in robes. All of them wore pendants of different kinds around their neck, and they all emanated auras of different colors. The person seated in the middle was the first to address him. There were no words spoken. The communication was purely telepathic.

The elder said, "Welcome home, Rikki, you have done well in this most recent lifetime of yours."

Rikki, hesitantly, said, "Thank you."

The elder said, "However, you have arrived early. None of your contemporaries are here yet."

Rikki said, "Well, my body was severely injured in an accident. It is now in a coma, and I'm not certain I'd like to dwell in it, as mangled as it appears to be."

The elders appeared to converse for a few moments and then the one who sat in the middle addressed him again. "This will not be a meeting for a review of your lifetime, as is normal in these circumstances. We will wait and do that at another time. This will instead be a celebration, a chance for you to meet formally with your over-soul. Now, let it be."

The council elder gestured with his arms stretched wide, and Old Soul stepped forward. In this instant Rikki, recognized that he himself was one and the same as Old Soul. His over-soul was Old Soul; he had been his own guide throughout his entire lifetime.

The elder continued, "Normally you would join with your over-soul at this time and meld together, yet retaining your individuality; as have all the souls he has sent out on previous occasions, some of which you have already recalled as your own past lives. But since you have arrived early, we'd like to extend an offer for you to return to your physical body. We will assist you in repairing the injuries to your body, and you will, from this day forward, be fully cognizant of your over-soul, who has been your spiritual guide, or fylgja, as you have preferred to refer to him, up until now."

Rikki replied, "Thank you. I'd like a few more years, provided my body functions fairly normally."

In that instant, a porthole opened within the council hall, and Rikki could see where his body lay on the hospital bed. The council elders joined in prayer as they focused their healing energy toward the body, and Rikki could see that his vital signs began to return to normal.

The elder said, "The time is now, Rikki. Step into the porthole, and join with your body. We will finish the job after your soul is secure within its confines."

Rikki stepped into the vortex, and, within an instant, he found himself lodged within his familiar physical body again as he regained consciousness, in pain but fully alert. It had been a near-death experience, through which all the trepidations of physical existence had vanished in an instant.

Recommended Reading

Frankl, Victor. *Man's Search For Meaning.* New York: Washington Square Press, 1959.

Frankl, Victor. *Psychotherapy and Existentialism.,* New York: Washington Square Press,1985.

Frankl, Victor. *The Will To Meaning: Foundations And Applications Of Logotherapy.* New York: Penguin Books, 1969.

Frankl, Victor. *Man's Search For Ultimate Meaning.* New York: Plenum Press, 1997.

Lucas, Elizabet. *Meaning In Suffering: Comfort In Crisis Through Logotherapy.* Berkeley: Institute Of Logotherapy Press, 1986.

Lucas, Elizabet._*Logotherapy Textbook.* Munich: Profil Verlag, 1998.

Newton, Michael. *Journey Of Souls. St. Paul:* Llewellyn Publications, 1994.

Newton, Michael. *Destiny Of Souls. St. Paul:* Llewellyn Publications, 2000.

Newton, Michael._*Life Between Lives*. St. Paul: Llewellyn Publications 2004.

Roberts, Jane. *The Seth Material.* New York: Prentice-Hall, 1970.

Roberts, Jane. *Seth Speaks: The Eternal Validity Of the Soul.* New York: Prentice-Hall, 1972.

Roberts, Jane. *The Nature Of Personal Reality.* New York: Prentice-Hall, 1974.

Roberts, Jane. *The Unknown Reality.* Vol.1. New York: Prentice-Hall, 1977.

Roberts, Jane. *The Unknown Reality.* Vol.2, part 1. New York: Prentice-Hall, 1977

Roberts, Jane. *The Unknown Reality.* Vol.2, part 2. New York: Prentice-Hall, 1977

Roberts, Jane. *The Nature Of The Psyche: Its Human Expression.* New York: Prentice-Hall, 1979.

Roberts, Jane. *The Individual And The Nature Of Mass Events.* New York: Prentice-Hall, 1981.

Roberts, Jane. *Dreams Evolution, And Value Fulfillments. Vol. 1.* New York: Prentice-Hall, 1986.

Roberts, Jane. *Dreams Evolution, And Value Fulfillments. Vol. II.* New York: Prentice-Hall, 1986.

Roberts, Jane. *The Early Sessions, Vol 1-9.* Manhasset: New Awareness Network, 1997.

CPSIA information can be obtained at www.ICGtesting.com
Printed in the USA
LVOW090741260412

279162LV00004B/6/P